Dunfermline
The Post-War Years

Dunfermline
The Post-War Years

by Bert McEwan

breedon **books**
PUBLISHING

First published in Great Britain in 2004 by
The Breedon Books Publishing Company Limited
Breedon House, 3 The Parker Centre,
Derby, DE21 4SZ.

ISBN 1 85983 407 8

Printed and bound by Butler & Tanner,
Frome, Somerset, England.

Jacket printed by Lawrence-Allen Colour Printers,
Weston-super-Mare, Somerset, England.

CONTENTS

Dedication

To my wife Betty
For her tolerance, patience
and proof-reading,
and for not carrying out her
threat of leaving if I ever
bought a computer.

Acknowledgements

It would not have been possible to assemble the collection of photographs used in this book without the co-operation and assistance of a number of people. I wish to thank the management and staff of the Dunfermline Carnegie Library Local History Department for their assistance in locating suitable photographs for this publication, making special mention of Chris Neale, whose knowledge of the contents of the local History Collection is phenomenal. Photographs marked D.C.L. are from the Library Collection that includes (M.A.) the Morris Allan negatives, (N) Norval negatives and (E.M.C.) slides from the Edith May Collection. The Fife Council Museum Service (F.M.S.) also gave access to their collection held at Viewfield Terrace. My thanks are also due to the Chief Executive Officer, management and staff of the Dunfermline Press Group (D.P.G.) who allowed me to inspect the Photographic Log of the Group covering the post-war era and select a number of suitable photographs, of which they retain ownership and copyright, from their extensive archives. The friendly advice and assistance given by the Dunfermline Press Group photographers was greatly appreciated. I am grateful to the people who have allowed me to use photographs, either loaned to me or donated by them to the Library Collection, and I have endeavoured to give attribution to the authors, where known, of all of the photographs used. To any who have been missed I can only apologise. I would like to thank all who have helped in any way to make this book possible.

INTRODUCTION

VE DAY. *D.C.L. (A. Cunningham)*
The caption for this photograph is VE Day but it is more likely to have been taken on the evening of the day following, 9 May, which had been a public holiday, as people would appear to be making their way towards the Public Park where there was a bonfire, entertainment and a night of celebrating the end of the war in Europe. The war in the Far East continued until the surrender of Japan on 2 September 1945.

ENGAGEMENTS. *D.P.G.*
The end of the war meant that people could once more make plans for their future. This led to a deluge of engagements and weddings. Bob and Betty Thomson were photographed in 1995 celebrating the 50th anniversary of their engagement on VE Day.

The origin and past history of the City and Royal Burgh of Dunfermline, ancient capital of Scotland, birthplace and burial place of royals, has been visited and revisited with a greater or lesser degree of accuracy in the many volumes that have been published over the past two centuries.

Less emphasis has been placed in recent publications on the life and times of Dunfermline and its residents in the period from the end of World War Two to the present date. It is the aim of this book to remedy this and to portray scenes, events and aspects of life which are probably within the lifetime of the reader and which will stir memories, happy and sad, of life in the Dunfermline area over the past 60 years. This period covers the years of my working life, much of which was spent in and around Dunfermline. While I

have tried to cover each aspect of the past in themed sections, it will be obvious that many of these overlap. For instance the Carnegie Dunfermline Trust has influence in Sport and the alterations to the Roads and Streets in Dunfermline have in turn influenced Shopping and Housing. Some photographs could have appeared in a number of the sections but their eventual location, I hope, has some relevance.

It is hoped that many questions will be answered about 'what was there before?' and not too many arguments will be started on 'I remember when'.

I apologise for any mistakes made in the recalling of events or the wrong titling or dating of photographs. Some can be blamed on memory loss while others will have been made because wrong information has been attached to the photographs used from various archives. While these archives are extensive it is frustrating that many events, buildings and people do not appear to have been photographed. The Local History Department of the Carnegie Library is always grateful for donations of photographs, writings and memorabilia relating to the City and Royal Burgh of Dunfermline and its citizens.

WEDDINGS. *D.P.G.*
Bert Jones and his wife were photographed celebrating their golden wedding in 1995, having been married in 1945. Bert is a prominent member of the Normandy Veterans' Association.

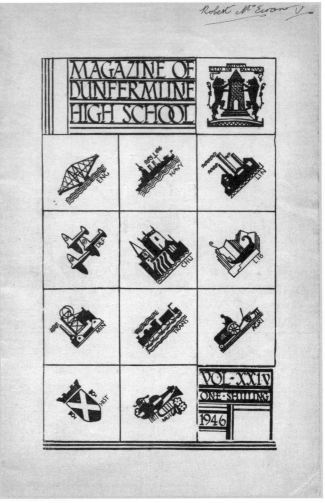

DUNFERMLINE HIGH SCHOOL MAGAZINE. *Anon.*
This is the cover of the 1946 Dunfermline High School Magazine, the first to be published after the complete end of hostilities in World War Two. It contained a Roll of Honour of those former pupils who had been killed and a welcome to the members of staff who had returned to teach after serving in the Armed Forces. Mr J.G. Lindsay is congratulated on being awarded the OBE for services to teaching.

And what of the pupils in this year 1946? How do they compare with the pre-war vintage? Or perhaps it would be safer to put it this way, how do they differ? For they have changed, in my view, though in a way difficult to define. That, of course, is only to be expected. One cannot go through a long war unscathed, and we are participating in a complete social revolution. And so I find the pupils to-day coming to school with a slightly different equipment and outlook. We still get our quota of bright pupils, and, in spite of what we often say and think, the pupils are not getting less intelligent. In the realm of Sport, matches are still played, and won or lost as heretofore, and everyone looks fit enough (while, of course, the Hall on Party night is as fine a picture of youth and beauty as ever it was!). I think the difference lies rather in a change of emphasis on what is considered important. While there are welcome signs of broader interests and a wider outlook on world affairs, I see right through the school an impatience to grow up at all costs, to be men and women as soon as possible, with their attendant liberties and privileges, but not always their responsibilities. Is there not a danger that in striving thus soon to ape their elders they may mistake the trappings and externals of manhood and womanhood for the reality, and lose that glowing zest of youth which is surely Nature's greatest boon? Do I imagine all this?

In any case I am confident that the youth of D.H.S. can and will face all problems squarely as in the past, and that D.H.S. will always be a good school to come back to!

W. F. L.

DUNFERMLINE HIGH SCHOOL MAGAZINE. *W.F. Lindsay.*
This is an extract from the 1946 Dunfermline High School Magazine that gives the views of a teacher returning to the school after war service in the Far East. It details his observations on the changes brought about by the war that had taken place during the past five years.

DUNFERMLINE HIGH SCHOOL. *D.C.L. (N.)*
This photograph, taken in 1945 or 1946, shows the members of the Dunfermline High School 2nd XI cricket team who would all be leaving school within the next two years to enter university or train in a trade or profession. The challenge of life in the post-war years lay before them. School pupils celebrating the end of the war in Europe painted VE signs on the doorway behind the players on 9 May 1945. The action cost one pupil his Prefect Badge. The paintwork was visible for many years.

CARNEGIE CLINIC EMERGENCY HOSPITAL. *D.P.G.*
For the duration of the war the Carnegie Clinic in Inglis Street was an Emergency Hospital. It was particularly busy in July and August 1944 after the D-Day landings in Normandy. Street collections were held in Dunfermline to raise funds to provide comforts for the wounded service personnel, some of whom were German soldiers. The *Dunfermline Journal* collected books and reading matter for the patients. A shield was presented by some of the soldiers as thanks for their generosity to the people of Dunfermline. Provost Les Wood is showing the shield that is kept in the City Chambers to former staff members at a reunion in 1983.

AIR RAID SHELTER. *D.P.G.*
Families who had sufficient garden space could apply for Anderson shelters that had to be half buried in the ground with the soil that had been removed being piled over the top as protection. People who had large houses with substantial floors could acquire a Morrison Shelter, a large 'table' designed to keep those under it safe from falling debris. Others were forced to use communal shelters built at various sites throughout Dunfermline. These took the form of reinforced basements, as was done under the Masonic Hall in Priory Lane, surface shelters built of brick and reinforced concrete, or brick and concrete shelters built in trenches in school playgrounds or in the parks and green spaces in the town. The latter two types were unpopular as they were located away from houses and it meant getting fully dressed before taking cover. There were very few daylight air-raid warnings for Dunfermline. After the war Anderson shelters were dug up and reused as garden sheds, while surface and buried shelters were demolished and the ground reinstated. The photograph shows a buried shelter that was located at the side of the roadway between Park Avenue and Comely Park being demolished in 1972. There are a number of places in the parks of Dunfermline where bumps and hollows can be seen marking the former location of shelters.

ANDERSON SHELTERS. *McEwan.*
At the end of the war, Anderson shelters that had been installed in the gardens in the Dunfermline area were quickly dug up and put to alternative uses. Some became the basis for garages but the most common use was as garden sheds, as shown at these allotments in Rosyth.

WARTIME BUILDING. *McEwan.*

This building built behind the City Chambers during the war may have been erected as decontamination centre, command post or shelter. It would appear that planning permission was not required for such buildings at that time and therefore there are no records showing its purpose. The windows may have been added at a later date to give it a new life. The site is such that it would have been buried with debris if a bomb had hit the City Chambers.

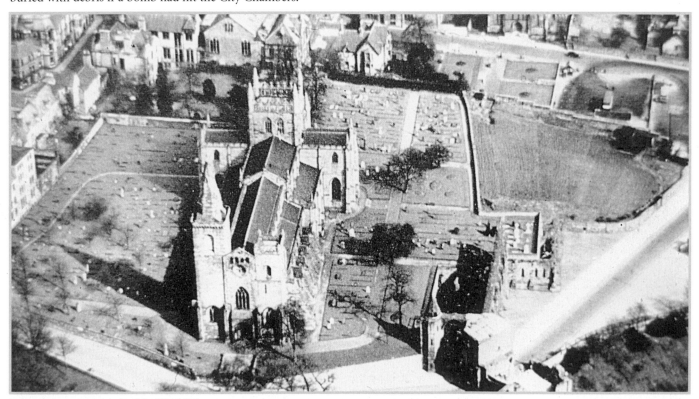

DUNFERMLINE ABBEY. *D.C.L. (E.M.C.)*

Little has changed in the historical heart of Dunfermline since this aerial photograph was taken *c.*1946. The St Andrew's South Church just visible at the top right has gone, as has the Lower Bus Station where buses left for Rosyth, Inverkeithing and the Fife coastal towns. The grassy area beside the bus station became the Garden of Remembrance and 1939–45 war memorial in 1953. Abbot House, to the left of the Abbey, would become a Heritage Centre in 1995.

DUNFERMLINE. *D.C.L. (M.A.)*
This aerial photograph, dated 1952, shows central Dunfermline from William Street in the west to Carnegie Hall in the east and from Nethertown in the south to Baldridgeburn in the north. Considering that 10 factory chimneys can be seen and the majority of the houses would still be burning coal, the photograph shows no sign of smoke pollution. Perhaps it was taken during the summer holiday shut down.

PITTENCRIEFF PARK. *D.C.L. (M.A.)*
The 1958 aerial photograph shows the extent of Pittencrieff Park. Also to be seen at the top right of the photograph are some of the factories that provided employment for the people of Dunfermline and West Fife at that time.

PUBLIC PARK. *D.C.I. (M.A.)*

This photograph, also taken in 1958, shows the other lung of Dunfermline, the Public Park. On the right side is the Upper Station with its large goods and coal yards while on the left side can be seen the Lower Railway Station that also had sidings where spare carriages were kept. At the top of the road access to the Lower Station there were huts that were used by the Racing Pigeon Club for the registration of entrants for races. The pigeons would be loaded into special baskets that would be put on a train to a predetermined destination where the birds would be released to race home to their owners. Motor traffic was allowed in the Public Park at this time and a car can be seen on the east carriageway. The area at the top right of the photograph would undergo a dramatic change in the coming 30 years.

LOCAL GOVERNMENT

For the first 30 years after the war the City and Royal Burgh of Dunfermline had a Town Council. Local government reorganisation was proposed to take effect in 1975. The first proposals were for the administration of the Kingdom of Fife to be split between Edinburgh and Dundee. There was great local opposition to this and demonstrations and rallies were held throughout the county. To the delight of the residents the proposal was dropped and Fife acquired a regional council. The old town councils were abolished and district councils were set up with the Dunfermline District Council being responsible for the area from Kincardine on Forth to Aberdour. Further reorganisation took place in 1996 when district councils were abolished and administration changed to Fife Council, who then took responsibility for all local matters. The administration headquarters for Fife Council is in Glenrothes. Planning matters are still dealt with locally. Community councils were set up for small areas and each council was allocated funds to cover the cost of administration and which could also be used for minor projects in the respective districts.

Some of the councils have been very successful in acting as pressure groups, keeping the main council informed of the thoughts and wishes of the electorate and in carrying out projects. Others have not survived due to lack of interest and the difficulty in finding office holders.

FIGHT FOR FIFE, 1971. *D.P.G.*
As part of the fight to keep Fife as an independent local authority, a motorcade was organised to gather support for the campaign and to show the feelings of the Fife electorate to the government.

'KIRKIN' OF THE COUNCIL, 1973. *D.C.L.*
Provost Les Wood, the Town Clerk, Baillies and Councillors being led from Dunfermline Abbey after the ceremonial 'Kirkin' of the Council in 1973. After the reorganisation of local government to form Fife Council the 'Kirkin' now takes place in churches throughout Fife.

DUNFERMLINE AND DISTRICT COUNCIL, *c.1980. D.C.L.*
Provost Les Wood with Councillors and senior Council officials on an official photograph taken in the 1980s.

ROSYTH PUBLIC LIBRARY. *D.C.L.*
The Dunfermline District Council built the Rosyth Library in 1988 when the one housed in part of the Rosyth Institute provided by the Carnegie Dunfermline Trust became inadequate for the increased population of the garden city.

THE CARNEGIE
DUNFERMLINE TRUST

The Trust was set up by Andrew Carnegie in 1903 to carry out good works and to administer Pittencrieff Park, given to the people of Dunfermline by him that year. The Trust Deed transferred the Park and $2,500,000 in bonds which would realise an income of £25,000. This money was to be used to bring 'sweetness and light' into the drab lives of the people of Dunfermline. Carnegie told the trustees 'remember you are pioneers, and do not be afraid of making mistakes: those who never make mistakes never make anything. Try many things freely, but discard just as freely'. Mr Carnegie gave a further £250,000 to the Trust in 1911.

The initiation of the welfare state and changes in state education after the war meant that many schemes which the Trust had implemented were now being provided by the taxpayer and the Trust could now withdraw its funding thus making monies available for new projects. Gradually over the years since the war the Trust has sold or transferred properties to the Dunfermline Town Council, Dunfermline District Council or Fife Council and other tenants. Many of the terms of sale include a reversion clause that means that if the property ceases to be used for its stated purpose then it will revert to the Trust.

With current assets of around £10 million giving an income of some £350,000 per annum, the Trust maintains its purpose by giving awards and grants to clubs, organisations and individuals for a wide variety of sport, education, art and heritage projects each year, details of which are published in the Trust Annual Report.

THE AMBITION FOUNTAIN. *McEwan.*

The figure of a boy holding aloft a wreath of laurels was sculpted by Richard Goulden who also sculpted the Andrew Carnegie Statue and the Fountain in the Music Pavilion. The inscription around the base of the figure 'Let Noble Ambition Be The True Thirst Of Youth Always' gives the fountain its name. Because it was vandalised on a number of occasion and the marble slabs around the base were stolen, the statue was removed from its position west of Pittencrieff House. After a number of years in secure storage the Carnegie Dunfermline Trust had a fibreglass copy made which stands in the Board Room at the offices of the Trust and the original was loaned to Lauder Learning College where it was erected in the foyer of the Business and Conference Centre.

FLORAL CLOCK, PITTENCRIEFF PARK. *D.C.L.*

A floral clock was presented to the Carnegie Dunfermline Trust by the Rotary Club of Dunfermline to mark the golden jubilee of the club in 1972. It was laid out and installed on the grass bank to the east of the Tea House. The clock was continually being vandalised and the decision was taken to remove it at the end of 1972. The same fate befell fountains that were installed in the two paddling pools.

GARDEN FOR THE BLIND. *McEwan.*

A garden, with plants selected for their texture and scent, was created for the benefit of the visually impaired immediately inside the Bridge Street entrance to Pittencrieff Park. It was laid out and constructed by members of the Dunfermline Horticultural Society under the guidance of the Society chairman Mr S. McEwan in 1975. The garden was removed when the refurbishment of the Louise Carnegie Gates was carried out and it was intended that a replacement garden would be provided. By 2004 this had not been done. The commemorative plaque was lost when alterations were carried out on the adjoining property.

Model Traffic Area. *McEwan.*
This area with a 'road layout' where children could be taught road safety was created inside the Pittencrieff Street entrance to the Park in 1950. The area was supervised and in the first six days 1,220 children made use of the facility. Due to lack of funding for staff it was closed by Fife Council at the end of the 1999 season.

Pittencrieff Park Gardens and Greenhouses. *D.C.L. (N)*
The teak and glass greenhouses were built in 1911 by the Carnegie Dunfermline Trust. They were replaced with modern aluminium and glass units in 1973 but plans for the regeneration of the park may mean that traditional greenhouses will once more house the exotic plant specimens.

PITTENCRIEFF PARK GREENHOUSES. *D.C.L. (N)*
Even a black and white photograph can give an impression of the profusion of colours and the fragrances visitors could experience on a walk through the greenhouses.

PITTENCRIEFF PARK, LILY POND. *D.C.L. (N)*
This garden area with a lily pond was created after the stable block of the estate burned down. In 1952 when the photograph was taken, the pond had a statue of Pan in its centre and there was a drinking fountain on the back wall. Both were stolen. Only the Pan statue was recovered, but it has never been returned to its position in the pond.

BAND OF THE ROYAL CORPS OF SIGNALS. *D.C.L. (N)*
The Band of the Royal Corps of Signals was very popular when they performed for many years in the bandstand in Pittencrieff Park. They visited Dunfermline for a season each year and their conductor became known as 'The King of the Glen'. There is no record of the audience's reaction to the singing of Vince Hill, seen here as a bandsman with the band in 1954.

BAND PERFORMANCE, PITTENCRIEFF PARK. *D.C.L. (N)*
This was the size of audience that a band could expect when performing in Pittencrieff Park. A charge was made for seating and programmes were sold. Eventually a fence was erected to ensure that everyone did pay for the privilege of a seat. This performance in 1954 would appear to be a junior talent competition organised by the band of the Royal Corps of Signals during their week in Dunfermline.

BILLY THE COCKATOO, PITTENCRIEFF PARK. *D.C.L. (M.A.)*
A favourite resident in the aviary in Pittencrieff Park was Billy, a white cockatoo photographed in 1964. Children particularly liked him because he accepted money from them and hid it in gaps in the bricks around his cage. This money added up to a substantial sum each year and was given to charity.

CARNEGIE JUNIOR CHOIR. *D.C.L. (N)*
The Carnegie Junior Choir took part in many competitions and are photographed with their teacher, Mrs Elaine Brown, holding one of the awards that they won in 1973.

CHILDREN'S FLOWER SHOW. *McEwan.*

The Carnegie Dunfermline Trust supplies bulbs to school children at cost price and in the spring of each year, a Flower Show and Art Exhibition is held in the Music Pavilion of Pittencrieff Park at which the children can show off their abilities at growing and drawing flowers. The photograph was taken at the event in 1999. Many people will have memories of planting the bulbs in the bulb fibre supplied, putting them under beds and in dark cupboards to get them started and then willing the plants to flower at the exact time for the show. The whole process ends in tears of joy or frustration at the final judging of their efforts.

CARNEGIE YOUTH CENTRE THEATRE. *D.C.L. (M.A.)*

The Carnegie Dunfermline Trust converted the Women's Centre in Pilmuir Street, which they owned, into a Youth Centre that opened in 1947. The building had a large function hall that became the Skibo Theatre in 1953. The Youth Centre had a very active amateur dramatic group which staged shows such as *Bunty Pulls The Strings*, the 1951 cast of which is shown complete with live dog and his master, whose beard looks less than convincing. The Youth Centre transferred to Tower House in 1963 and the building was sold to the Stakis Organisation, which converted it into the Belleville Hotel that operated for nearly 20 years before being sold to become Johnson's Bar, Club and Entertainment Centre.

TOWER HOUSE, EAST PORT. *D.P.G.*

Tower House became the home of the Carnegie Youth Club in 1963 after the former Youth Centre in Pilmuir Street was sold. The building had been erected as a folly in the grounds of Viewfield House and was included in the sale of Carnegie Hall and Viewfield House to Dunfermline Town Council two years later. The building was demolished to make way for a new vehicle entrance to the Carnegie Hall Complex and the Youth Club was relocated in part of Commercial School, which then was renamed Tower House. Tower House can still be seen painted above a gateway in East Port at the pedestrian access to Carnegie Hall.

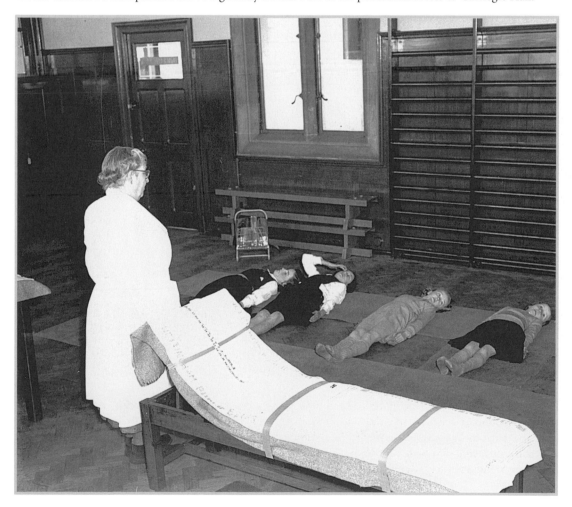

THE CARNEGIE CLINIC. *D.C.L. (N)*

One of a number of remedial clinics in the Carnegie Clinic, Inglis Street, in 1954. The Carnegie Dunfermline Trust maintained a responsibility for the treatment of children until 1958. There was a Dental Clinic whose dentist, Miss Leslie, probably put a whole generation of children off dentists for life. She had a philosophy that all baby teeth should be gone by the age of nine and endeavoured to give nature a helping hand with a pair of pincers.

JUNIOR SPORTS CUP. *D.C.L. (N)*
Townhill School were the first winners of the Junior Sports Cup awarded by the Carnegie Dunfermline Trust in 1958.

PITREAVIE RUNNING TRACK. *D.C.L. (M.A.)*
The Carnegie Dunfermline Trust improved facilities at Pitreavie playing fields by providing a running track. This had a cinder running surface and there was a changing hut for competitors.

OPENING OF THE NEW STAND AT PITREAVIE. *D.C.L. (N)*
In 1961 a new Stand was built at what would later be called the Pitreavie Athletics Stadium. The photograph of the opening ceremony shows trustees David Drysdale and Andrew Buchanan on the left and secretary and treasurer of the Trust, Fred Mann, on the right.

THE PITREAVIE RUNNING TRACK. *D.C.L. (N)*
This photograph taken in 1961 shows the track and the newly-built stand. It is the home of the Pitreavie Athletic Club and the facilities have continuously been upgraded, mainly with funding from the Carnegie Dunfermline Trust. The facilities have allowed local athletes to fulfil their potential at national and international events.

BENACHIE HOUSE AND CARNEGIE HALL. *McEwan.*

The Carnegie Hall complex of Benachie House, the Annexe and Carnegie Hall provides a base for music and drama in Dunfermline. Benachie House is where countless numbers of children have been taught singing or to play a musical instrument. The Annexe, which started life as a wooden hut but has now been replaced by a purpose-built performance area, was where dance classes and rehearsals for the brass bands, orchestras and choirs were held. The Carnegie Hall, with a seating capacity of around 500, is used by professional performers and amateur groups and can also function as a film theatre.

TAPESTRY WEAVING. *D.P.G.*

The Carnegie Dunfermline Trust has commissioned the weaving of a number of tapestries illustrating the history and heritage of Dunfermline. In 1981 William Wilson of Caithness designed a tapestry based on the lives of Malcolm Canmore and St Margaret. Here the completed work is shown with the volunteer weavers who interpreted his design. The tapestry can be seen hung in the Dunfermline Carnegie Library.

STAINED GLASS PANELS. *D.P.G.*

Shona McInnes of Inverurie was commissioned by the Carnegie Dunfermline Trust to design stained glass panels for the entrance of the new Queen Margaret Hospital. The panels depict the Dunfermline skyline and its road network. They were handed over to the hospital by Trust chairman Jessie Spittal in 1993.

DUNFERMLINE CRAFT SCHOOL. *D.C.L. (N)* Viewfield House was the home of the Carnegie Dunfermline Trust Craft School. In the school students, young and old, were taught weaving, woodwork, metalwork, leatherwork, jewellery making and artwork of all types to an exceptionally high standard and Pittencrieff Park Music Pavilion was the venue for displays of the students' work. The photograph shows some of the work displayed at the 1959 exhibition.

THE CARNEGIE FESTIVAL ORCHESTRA. *D.C.L. (N)*

A Festival of the Arts was sponsored by the Carnegie Dunfermline Trust for a number of years before being superseded by the Dunfermline District and later the Fife Arts Festivals. At the centre of the Festival was the Symphony Orchestra, whose members took part in workshops in local schools as well as performing in concerts with top international soloists. The 1971 orchestra is seen here rehearsing under its conductor Christopher Seaman.

LOCOMOTIVE NAMING CEREMONY. *D.C.L.*

During the 1985 celebrations to mark the 150th anniversary of the birth of Andrew Carnegie a British Rail locomotive was given the name *Andrew Carnegie*. Present at the ceremony was the millionaire's great-great-grandson. The locomotive worked from Inverness for a number of years.

HEALTH

The immediate post-war years were dominated by the setting up of the National Health Service. After 1948 all hospitals and health centres in the Dunfermline area, together with the Glenlomond Hospital for tuberculosis near Kinnesswood, came under the management of the West Fife Health Board which had its management offices in Comely Park.

The Carnegie Clinic was converted to a health centre in 1950 and in 1956 the Carnegie Dunfermline Trust handed over its medical welfare interests and school clinics to Dunfermline Town Council.

The Combination Home and Hospital in Leys Park Road, known locally as the Poorhouse, was converted into a medical hospital and reopened in 1953. It remained as such until 1967 when it was converted for the use of long-stay elderly patients, a service that it carried out until its closure in 1985. It was subsequently sold to be used as a residential home for the elderly.

The Dunfermline and West Fife Hospital was the principal surgical and medical hospital for the area. A new casualty block was built in 1958 and the main operating theatre was converted in 1966 to a twin theatre facility thus allowing more operations to be carried out. After extensive modernisation of wards

MILESMARK HOSPITAL. *D.C.L.*
The hospital was built as an Isolation and Infectious Diseases Hospital. When the need for such a facility decreased it was converted to become a medical hospital and some wards were converted for convalescent and geriatric purposes. The opening of the new Queen Margaret Hospital rendered it redundant. The walkways from the central building, the administration department and the nurses' home to the wards may have been covered, but they had no sides, making it a cold and sometimes wet walk going on and off duty. The buildings were demolished and the site cleared for house building. The Grounds and Gardens Department for the West Fife Hospital Group was based at the hospital and the greenhouses, cold frames and propagation beds can be seen on the left of this 1973 photograph.

NORTHERN HOSPITAL. *D.C.L.*
Now Leys Park Nursing Home, the property started life as the Dunfermline Poorhouse. It later became a Combination Hospital and Poorhouse before being transferred to the National Health Service in 1946 and converted into a medical hospital. It was closed in 1985 when the first phase of the new General Hospital opened and the building was sold and converted for its present purpose.

five and six in 1981 and 1983 respectively, new modular theatres were added in 1986. In 1994 after the Dunfermline and West Fife Hospital closed, the modular theatre unit was dismantled and transported to Romania where it was rebuilt. The project was carried out as a *Challenge Anneka*. This was a BBC television programme in which Anneka Rice recruited local volunteers to help her complete a challenge. The programme gave credit to the many local firms and organisations that helped and all of the work was carried out over a very tight timescale.

The building of a new general hospital to serve the West Fife area was commenced in 1981 with phase 1 being opened in 1985. Phase 2 was opened in 1993 by HRH Anne, the Princess Royal, and all patients and clinics from the Dunfermline and West Fife and Milesmark Hospitals were transferred to the new hospital.

Provision was made in the new building for maternity facilities but the Fife Health Board, which had been formed by the amalgamation of the former East and West Fife Boards, decided that these should now be centralised in Kirkcaldy. The Maternity Hospital in Izatt Avenue, which had been opened in 1937 and extended in 1943, 1969 and 1985, was now

redundant. The last birth in the hospital was in 1993. The building was sold and is now a centre for small businesses.

Milesmark Hospital was built as an isolation hospital for infectious diseases. Many local residents will remember the dreaded brown ambulance that came to pick up patients to be taken there. When the patient was cured he or she was taken home in a Wolesley car that was driven by the same Mr Johnston who had driven them in the ambulance. The need for a separate hospital for this purpose reduced with children receiving immunisation and the use of antibiotics and the hospital was, in 1967, converted to become an Acute Medical Unit with an outpatients department added in 1973. The hospital closed in 1993 and was demolished.

There had been four hospitals in Dunfermline but now there was now only one, which would cater for all the surgical and medical needs of the residents of West Fife. In 2002 the decision was taken by the Fife Health Board and endorsed by the Health Minister of the Scottish Parliament, that all in-patient and emergency trauma services should be provided at the Victoria Hospital in Kirkcaldy. This situation has not been accepted by the majority of people in Dunfermline and

DUNFERMLINE AND WEST FIFE HOSPITAL, NEW ROW. *D.C.L.*

After serving as the main emergency and surgical hospital for Dunfermline and West Fife for over 100 years, the hospital became redundant when the Queen Margaret hospital was built. The Dunfermline and West Fife site was sold and the majority of the buildings were demolished to make way for future development. After hopes were raised on a number of occasions by planning applications that came to nothing, work finally started in 2003 to build new office accommodation that would incorporate the old Cottage Hospital building. Fife Council will rent the new offices. This photograph was taken shortly before demolition of the hospital started. Priory House, on the right, will be retained and housing will be built on the remainder of the site.

DUNFERMLINE AND WEST FIFE HOSPITAL, REID STREET. *D.C.L.*

The photograph shows the main entrance of the Dunfermline and West Fife Hospital in Reid Street. The newer building on the right was for laboratory services.

West Fife and the fight to retain all services at the Queen Margaret Hospital goes on.

Princess Alexandra opened a new hospital specifically designed for patients with mental health problems at Lynebank in 1969. Since then the thinking on how such patients should be treated has changed and as patients have been returned to living in the community, wards have closed or been turned over to other nursing needs. It is the intention of the Health Board that the hospital should close when all of the patients have been relocated.

The introduction of the National Health Service meant that the load placed on GPs increased dramatically and coping with patients in a room that was part of a doctor's house was no longer an option. Practices took on more partners, which meant there was a need for more consulting rooms. The purpose-built doctors' surgery was born. Dr Burt and his partners moved from their New Row Surgery into part of Abbot House in the 1960s but were required to move to the new Millhill Surgery in 1990 when the practice outgrew the premises. Within 10 years even

DUNFERMLINE MATERNITY HOSPITAL. *D.C.L.*
The Maternity Hospital in Izatt Avenue was built just before the start of World War Two. It was extended and modernised on a number of occasions but the opening of the Queen Margaret Hospital and revised thinking by the Fife Health Board resulted in maternity services being transferred to Kirkcaldy despite a vigorous campaign being waged for its retention. The building was sold and is now a business centre.

FOD HOUSE PRE-NURSING SCHOOL, 1957. *D.C.L. (M.A.)*
The West Fife Hospitals Board had a Nursing School in Comely Park that provided classroom teaching to augment the training given to nurses in the group hospitals. A pre-nursing school was opened at Fod House to prepare potential nursing staff for hospital work. The school transferred to a new purpose-built college in Kirkcaldy and now takes students to graduate status.

that needed to be extended. The practice that had operated from a house in Viewfield Terrace moved to the Bellyeoman Surgery in 1986 and that too has been extended. The doctors who consulted in Comely Park moved to the New Park Surgery in Robertson Road and those in Park Avenue moved, first to the Nethertown and then to Elliot Street. Hospital Hill Surgery was built in Izatt Avenue to replace the one in the doctor's house in Aberdour Road. Rosyth now has a new surgery at Primrose Lane.

Pharmacies have opened up adjacent to most of the new surgeries. New health centres were built at Rosyth and Dalgety Bay in 1983 and 1984.

An ageing population has seen the need for residential care and sheltered housing increase rapidly. Fife Council own the Matthew Fyfe residential care home at Broomhead Drive and there are many privately-run homes in the area. Fife Council provide sheltered housing throughout Dunfermline and Rosyth while there have been several privately-built complexes of retirement homes developed in recent years.

WEST FIFE HOSPITALS BOARD OF MANAGEMENT. *D.C.L.*
The photograph was taken to mark the end of the West Fife Hospitals Board in 1974 and shows the members who had served since the inception of the Board in 1948. The Board was not politically driven and consisted of members of the community and the medical profession whose aim was the betterment of the health of the people of West Fife. William M. Muir, who was secretary and treasurer of the Board for the whole period, is seated first left and the Dowager Countess of Elgin is in the centre of the front row.

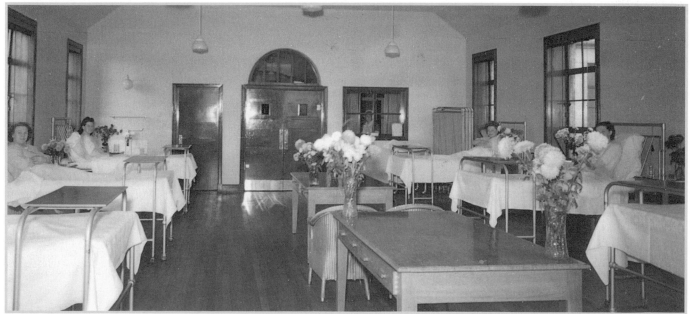

MATERNITY HOSPITAL. *D.C.L. (M.A.)*
The photograph was taken in 1951 and shows some of the new mothers in one of the 'Nightingale' style wards in the hospital.

HOSPITAL ENTERTAINMENT. *D.C.L. (M.A.)*
Artists who were performing at Carnegie hall and at the Opera House regularly entertained hospital patients and staff. At Christmas the staff, medical and ancillary, showed their many talents at concerts in two of the wards. The photograph shows patients, staff and visitors being entertained by a visiting pipe band. Was this an early answer to bed blocking?

CHALLENGE ANNEKA. *D.P.G.*
When the Dunfermline and West Fife Hospital closed, one of the surgeons suggested that the theatres and equipment could be sent to an Eastern European country. The transfer was agreed but fell through due to lack of facilities to carry out the work. A television programme named *Challenge Anneka* carried out projects which had to be completed in a fixed time and the producers took up the challenge to dismantle the theatres and equipment, transport it to Romania where the theatres were rebuilt and made functional again. Anneka Rice fronted the programme and was responsible for arranging the necessary labour and equipment from local contractors whose only reward was the publicity gained and the knowledge that a needy community would gain a valuable asset. There were many eager fans who came to see the work being done and lend a hand. These two young fans only wanted autographs.

VIEWFIELD SURGERY. *McEwan.*

This building was the home and surgery of Doctors Cairncross, Tomkinson and Frater before the practice moved to a new purpose built surgery at Bellyeoman Road in 1986. The room on the right was the waiting room and many patients will remember that when traffic passed along East Port or up Viewfield Terrace the glass in the door vibrated.

HOSPITAL HILL SURGERY, IZATT AVENUE. *D.C.L.*

This surgery was built as a replacement for the one located in the doctor's house in Aberdour Road.

SOCIAL AND WELFARE

Changes in lifestyle, housing and the use of leisure time have all contributed to the change in needs for the residents of Dunfermline. When houses did not have bathrooms people used the facilities that were provided at the various institutes, built by the Carnegie Dunfermline Trust in the first two decades of the 20th century.

These institutes, located at Townhill, Baldridgeburn, Nethertown and Rosyth, had reading rooms, games rooms, meeting rooms, a large function room and showers and slipper baths, all of which were used by the residents of the surrounding areas. One object of the Carnegie Dunfermline Trust when it was set up by

Andrew Carnegie was to initiate and develop ideas and to provide the initial funding for these ideas. It was with this in mind that the Trust took the decision in 1946 to hand over the institutes to the Dunfermline Town Council.

The same policy saw the Carnegie Hall, Music Institute, Craft School, Dalgety House, Tower House and the Dunfermline Museum sold to the Town Council in 1965. The administration and maintenance of Pittencrieff Park was transferred to the Dunfermline District Council in 1976. Transitional funding was provided by the Trust for a number of years. These changes in direction allowed the Trust to direct its

CHAPEL STREET, c.1965. D.C.L.
Dunfermline had at least three model lodging houses providing sleeping, frequently dormitory-style, and communal cooking facilities for their clients. They had originally been built to house the hundreds of labourers who moved to the area to work on the building of the railway lines throughout Fife and the building of the Forth Railway Bridge. Further work came to the area when the government decided to locate the Naval Dockyard at Rosyth and the lodging houses were used by workers until 'Tintown' was erected near to the base to accommodate them and their families. By the beginning of World War Two the largest of them, on the corner of Bruce Street and Chapel Street, had closed. The two on the north side of Chapel Street continued to be used by itinerant labourers until the nearest building, owned by Jenny Rintoul, closed and was let out as offices before finally being demolished, followed in around 1972 by the second building which was owned by John McDonald. No longer would the smell of frying kippers greet passers-by in Chapel Street on a Friday night.

TAM DEVLIN, DUNFERMLINE WORTHY, 1984. *D.C.L. (E.M.C.)* Over the years Dunfermline has had its share of worthies, Johnny Purvis and Buck both of whom sold evening papers outside the Kinema and Regal and Bobby Brown who was just himself. He was renowned for breaking the windows of properties in Kirkgate when refused accommodation in the Kirkgate Police Station thus ensuring that he would be given a bed in a cell for the night. When sentenced to imprisonment, Bobby would guide newly-recruited policemen to Saughton Jail in Edinburgh and keep them right on all the procedures necessary during the transfer. All the worthies were harmless and well known. Tam Devlin lived rough in the Urquhart Farm area for many years and could be seen wandering around the various premises in town where he knew that he would get something to eat and drink. In the photograph he is seen in Chalmers Street having been provided with sustenance, probably by Stephen's bakery. Every so often he would have a bath, perhaps unwillingly, and be given fresh clothes by a welfare group. There are now *Big Issue* sellers and a number of visiting buskers in Dunfermline but none of them seem to be 'characters' like the old worthies.

resources to other causes and widen the scope of its activities.

At one time Dunfermline had three model lodging houses but by the end of the war only two were still in use. These were located in the Chapel Street area and provided accommodation for men in dormitory-style rooms with communal kitchen and toilet facilities. They had been built for the influx of labour required for the building of the Forth Railway Bridge and the Rosyth Naval Dockyard in the latter part of the 19th and early years of the 20th century. The last lodging house closed and was demolished in around 1972 and the remaining residents, some of whom had lived there for many years, found alternative places to live.

Town Councils were required to provide facilities for the recreational needs of the residents of the housing schemes around Dunfermline and Community Centres were built at Abbeyview (complete with bowling green), Paton Street, Kingseat and Rosyth.

EDUCATION

The new building for the Dunfermline High School had been opened in St Leonard's Place in 1939, shortly before the outbreak of war. This meant that the old High School building in Priory Lane was available and Queen Anne School moved in, thus vacating part of the building in Reform Street to which Canmore Primary School moved. This allowed Queen Anne School to also take over the old Canmore building adjacent to the Old High School. This shifting around gave the schools sufficient capacity until the post-war baby boom took effect at the beginning of the 1950s.

Facilities for secondary education at Queen Anne School became inadequate and space was at a premium, so a new complex was built at Venturefair in 1958. This has also proved to be too small and a new school built under a Public Private Partnership scheme opened in 2003.

An additional junior secondary school was required. It was first established in the former Queen Anne School building in Priory Lane and given the name Woodmill. The school moved to new premises in Shield's Road that opened in 1960. Pupils from the school graduated to Dunfermline High School at the end of the second year of studies. With the introduction of comprehensive education in 1968 the name was changed to Woodmill High School. The school was extended in 1972 and became a Community School in 1974 when the public were given access to the facilities in the evenings and at weekends.

Dunfermline High School also suffered from overcrowding and the building has acquired a number of extensions. This too became a Community School. The need for a new Catholic high school resulted in the building of St Columba's High School in 1969 to house pupils from all over West Fife.

King's Road School, Rosyth, was a junior secondary school until changing to junior high school with the

KING'S ROAD SCHOOL ROSYTH, 1976. *D.C.L. (E.M.C.)*
King's Road School was used as a junior secondary school when first built but when Inverkeithing High School opened pupils transferred to there and King's Road became a primary school. It was severely damaged by fire in 2001 and a replacement building opened in 2004.

introduction of comprehensive education and in 1972 the pupils moved to the newly-built Inverkeithing High School and King's Road reverted to primary school status in 1974. The introduction of comprehensive education put all of the senior schools in Dunfermline on an equal footing.

The Lauder Technical College, which had premises in Priory Lane and New Row, moved to a new complex at Halbeath in 1970 in order to accommodate the influx of students brought about by the increased need for technical tuition. Since then various extensions have been built and the college is linked to the Dunfermline Business Learning and Conference Centre on the same site.

The building of housing schemes and the subsequent movement of population meant that the primary schools were in the wrong place for their pupils and new primary schools needed to be built in more appropriate locations.

Blacklaw Primary was the first in 1953, followed by Camdean in the same year and Pitcorthie Primary School two years later. Linburn Primary opened in 1961. Touch Primary School, which opened in 1970, was the last school to be built using imperial measurements. Pitreavie Primary School opened in the same year.

Because of the fall in town centre population the Education Authority decided in 1958 to merge Canmore and Commercial primary schools. However, with the merger came the need for a more modern building and two new schools on a single site with shared sports facilities to house Commercial School and St Margaret's Catholic Primary School were built on part of Transy estate in 1970. The name Canmore was revived for an additional school on the Pitcorthie Estate in 1975. A new primary school was built for the children of Crossford in 1974 which meant no more walking along a busy main road to the old school that served pupils from Crossford and Cairneyhill and was sited halfway between the two villages. This ended the school building programme until 1998 when Bellyeoman Primary School at Robertson Road was opened.

The Lynebank and Headwell schools were opened to cater for children with special needs, Headwell in 1957 and Lynebank some 11 years later. Lynebank, which had been attached to Lynebank Hospital, was replaced by a purpose-built school in the hospital grounds and renamed the Robert Henryson School. It is the intention of Fife Council to provide a new building within the eastern development to house the pupils from both schools.

CANMORE PRIMARY SCHOOL, *c.1960*. *D.C.L.*
The school in Reform Street was built to house Queen Anne Secondary School. In 1940 a property swap saw Canmore Primary School move from its premises in the New Row to this building. St Margaret's Primary School also used part of the premises. Canmore and Commercial schools merged and moved to a new building on the Transy Estate, sharing playing fields with St Margaret's Primary School that also moved there. The site was acquired for the Kingsgate Shopping Centre Project and the school and the adjacent Opera House were demolished.

WYMET COURT. *McEwan.*
This building was erected as a primary feeder for the Dunfermline High School and was later renamed Canmore Primary School. After the school moved to Reform Street the building became part of the Queen Anne Secondary School complex. It was used by the Lauder Technical College from 1958 after Queen Anne School moved to the new school at Venturefair. In 1976, after the Lauder College was relocated in the new Technical College at Halbeath, the building was sold and converted into dwelling houses.

PARK ROAD SCHOOL ROSYTH, 1976. *D.C.L. (E.M.C.)*
During World War Two the Royal Air Force occupied the school.

PRIMARY SCHOOL CLASS, PARK ROAD SCHOOL, ROSYTH, *c*.1955. *D.C.L. (E.M.C.)*
The boys and girls of one of the classes at Park Road Primary School *c*.1955.

PITCORTHIE PRIMARY SCHOOL, 1970. *D.C.L.*
The creation of a large housing estate on the farmlands of East and West Pitcorthie meant that a new primary school was required to serve the families in that area. Pitcorthie Primary School was built in 1955.

PITREAVIE PRIMARY SCHOOL. *D.C.L.*
The shift of population from the town centre to the new housing estates at Abbeyview and Aberdour Road meant that new schools were required in these areas. Pitreavie Primary and Touch Primary schools were built in 1970.

ST MARGARET'S AND COMMERCIAL PRIMARY SCHOOLS. *D.C.L.*
The old school buildings in East Port and Holyrood Place were cramped and unsuitable for modern teaching methods. Fife County Council decided to adopt a radical concept of two schools being built adjacent to one another and sharing the same playing fields. The first project of this kind was the building of new schools to house the pupils from St Margaret's and Commercial Primary Schools on a greenfield site at Transy. The schools opened in 1970.

PRIMARY SCHOOL CLASS, COMMERCIAL SCHOOL, 1949-50. *D.C.L.*
A class from Commercial Primary School, 1949–50. The three girls seated third, fourth and fifth from the left are the Kent triplets.

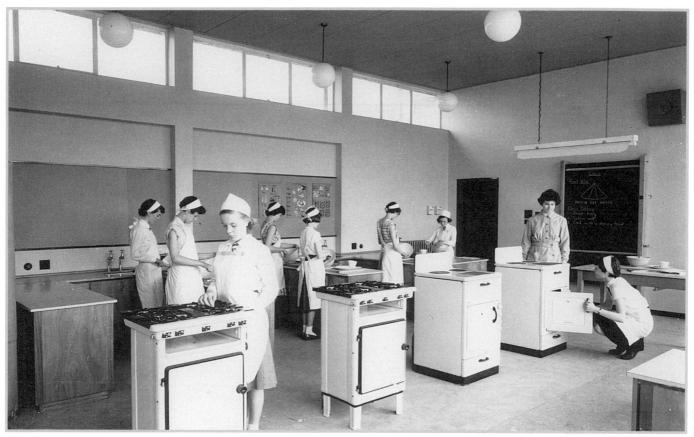

QUEEN ANNE SCHOOL. *D.C.L. (M.A.)*
Girls being taught Domestic Science, later named Home Economics, using the modern equipment in the new Queen Anne School in 1958.

QUEEN ANNE SCHOOL. *D.C.L. (M.A.)*
Boys learning to develop engineering skills with up-to-date equipment in the new metalwork room at Queen Anne School in 1958.

WOODMILL HIGH SCHOOL. *D.C.L. (M.A.)*
In 1974 the kitchens and dining room of Woodmill High School were refurbished.

CONTINENTAL VISITS. *D.C.L.*
A group of Dunfermline High School boys with their teacher, Alex McLennan, in the centre of the back row, are photographed at the Palace of Versailles on a visit to France in the early 1950s. These visits became an essential part of the school year.

RELIGION

The years since World War Two have seen a steady decline in membership of the established churches in and around Dunfermline. In an effort to maintain membership, some congregations moved to the centres of population from their old established city centre sites and other congregations formed unions to retain their viability.

The membership of St John's Church in Bruce Street united with that of St Columba's in Canmore Street to become St Paul's Parish Church in 1958 and the joint congregation worshipped in the Canmore Street church until it was destroyed by fire in 1976, when they then shared the Canmore Congregational Church with its members until 2000. St Paul's Church was disbanded on the retirement of their minister, Rev Frank Smith. St John's Church became a furniture warehouse before eventually plans were submitted for it to be converted into a hotel and nightclub in 2003.

The Canmore Congregational, now the United Reform Church, was itself the result of a union in 1974 with the North Congregational Church that was located in Pilmuir Street. The latter church became a carpet warehouse before being demolished in the late 1980s.

The St Andrew's Erskine congregation was formed firstly by a pre-war union of Chalmers Street and Queen Anne Street churches to form Erskine Church and then a further union with St Andrew's Parish Church in Chapel Street to become St Andrew's Erskine Parish Church in 1974. In 1996 the members took the decision to relocate to a new site at Robertson Road and the Queen Anne Street church building was sold. The erection of the new church building commenced in 2003. The St Andrew's Parish Church building became an auction house before being demolished in 1987.

St Andrew's South Parish Church that stood in St Margaret's Street, opposite the present car parks, relocated to Whitelaw Road and was renamed St Ninian's. The congregation first met in a wooden hut at the west end of the road and the minister, Douglas Beck, visited every house in the Abbeyview housing scheme as tenants moved in and so built up the congregation, which moved into the new hall church which was built on the top of the hill in 1957. That served until sufficient funds were raised to allow for the erection of a separate church on the adjoining site in 1966.

The design of this building was typical 1960s with a flat roof. Maintenance problems became such that the building was demolished in around 1993 and alterations were carried out to the 1957 building to make it suitable for use once more as a church. While this work was being carried out a fire gutted the

ST MARGARET'S PARISH CHURCH, 1972. *D.C.L.*
The congregation of St Margaret's Parish Church relocated to a new church building in the Touch housing estate and in 1981 the site was cleared to allow the building of a new headquarters and branch office of the Dunfermline Building Society. The Society's headquarters subsequently moved to new premises on the Carnegie Campus at Pitreavie in 1994.

building and a completely new hall church had to be built. The former St Andrew's South Church was used as a market hall until it was gutted by fire in 1977 and eventually demolished to allow the site to be used for housing.

St Margaret's Parish Church stood on a valuable site between East Port and James Street and a decision was taken to realise this asset and relocate the congregation in the new housing scheme at Touch. The move took place in 1974 and the former church was demolished to allow new headquarters to be built for the Dunfermline Building Society.

The increase in population in the southern area of Dunfermline brought a need for an additional Roman Catholic church and Our Lady of Lourdes Church opened in Aberdour Road in 1966.

While Rosyth lost one of its churches with the closure and subsequent demolition of the Church of St Andrew and St George, Albert Street, in 1986, new churches were built nearer to the naval family housing adjacent to the dockyard.

St Andrew's Church was dedicated in 1946, St Columba's Church opened in 1970, a Methodist church in 1971 and St Margaret's in 1969, but this church closed in 1996 when the naval personnel left the dockyard.

Several buildings throughout Dunfermline have been built or adapted for use by other religious sects over the past 50 years including the formation of a Mosque in the former Woodmill Miners' Social Club and the conversion of a former lemonade factory into a church for the Vine Fellowship.

ST ANDREW'S PARISH CHURCH, *c.*1976. *D.C.L.*
The congregations of St Andrew's Parish Church and Erskine Church decided in 1974 to unite and use the former Erskine Church buildings in Queen Anne Street. The redundant St Andrew's Church building was sold to become an auction house before it was demolished in 1987 to make way for the new Co-operative Supermarket that never opened for business and was itself demolished in 2004. On the right of the photograph is the Co-operative Pharmacy, the 'Store' Chemist, which was relocated in Randolph Street.

Religion

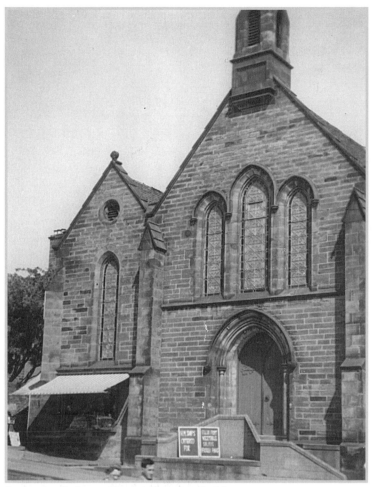

ST ANDREW'S SOUTH PARISH CHURCH. *D.C.L.*
St Andrew's South Parish Church was translated to the Abbeyview housing estate and renamed St Ninian's. The former church building became a market run by Thomas Black before being severely damaged in a fire that resulted in its demolition. The relevance of the wording on one of the signs saying that HM ships can be catered for, is that the market was directly opposite the Lower Bus Station where buses ran to and from the naval dockyard at Rosyth.

ST MARGARET'S ANGLICAN CHURCH, ROSYTH, *c.*1986. *D.C.L. (Mary Kidd).*
This wooden sculpture of St Margaret was carved in Orkney *c.*1986. It was shipped to Rosyth on board HMS *Orkney* and installed in St Margaret's Anglican Church. When the church closed the sculpture was removed and transferred to the naval church in Faslane that has been dedicated to St Margaret.

ST MARGARET'S ANGLICAN CHURCH, ROSYTH, 1993. *D.C.L. (Martin Rogers).*
The Anglican church with its distinctive roof was dedicated to St Margaret. It was built near to the naval base to serve the naval staff and their families in Rosyth. It was built to the north of the dockyard and was used by the community until after the departure of the minesweeper squadron from Rosyth in 1995 when it was closed and was sold to a commercial enterprise.

CATHOLIC PILGRIMAGE, 1964. *D.C.L. (M.A.)* For many years Catholic pilgrimages to the Shrine of St Margaret took place in Dunfermline. After a Mass at East End Park, pilgrims would walk to the site of the Shrine of St Margaret, which is to the east of Dunfermline Abbey.

RETIREMENT OF DOUGLAS BECK, 1971. *D.P.G.* Rev Douglas Beck was appointed to St Ninian's Parish Church when it was established to serve the Abbeyview housing estate. It is said that he walked around the estate in all weathers and visited every house as they became occupied, inviting the tenants to his church. The first church building was a wooden hut at the junction of Blacklaw Road and Whitelaw Road. The congregation moved to a hall church that was built between Duncan and Allan Crescents and this was used until a purpose-built church was erected. Matters moved a full circle when the church was abandoned and demolished due to maintenance difficulties with the flat roof and the congregation once again worships in a hall church. Douglas Beck retired in 1971.

ROADS AND RAILWAYS

Generally, new roads and streets have been created as and when required by housing, commercial or industrial development on the various estates around Dunfermline. The most obvious major changes to the road network of the town have been the widening and extension of Carnegie Drive to Sinclair Gardens in 1973, the construction of the Eastern Link Road, St Margaret's Drive, from Bothwell Gardens through the public park to Sinclair Gardens in 1988, and the upgrading to dual carriageway of Hospital Hill and St Leonard's Street in 2000.

Nethertown Broad Street was widened to four lanes with a view to this being carried on around the south and west sides of Pittencrieff Park to create a ring road, but the abandonment of the western development has, at least temporarily, put this on hold. The very necessary Appin Crescent bypass is still eagerly awaited.

The building of a new bus station at James Street allowed all of the bus services to terminate at one site and the lower bus station in St Margaret's Street and the Carnegie Street bus station both became redundant. All local bus services also pass along James Street, making the connection between town and country easier.

The growth of car ownership and the need to travel from the housing estates on the edges of the town meant that the ever-increasing demand for car parking was relentless. The James Street and Kingsgate developments included a multi-storey car park and vacant areas of ground at Viewfield Terrace, Walmer Drive, Carnegie Drive and Bruce Street were all converted to car parks, as was the lower bus station.

A major scheme to fill in the ravine of the Tower Burn using the waste from the pit bing at Wellwood was undertaken from 1966–8. This then allowed the Chalmers Street car park to be formed and also provided much needed rear access to some of the properties in Bruce Street, Bridge Street and Chalmers Street.

THE FORTH ROAD BRIDGE. *D.C.L. (M.A.)* Two wonders of the modern world side by side. An aerial view of the Forth Road Bridge and the approach road almost completed. The opening ceremony would be performed by Her Majesty the Queen on 4 September 1964.

Many well known and loved streets disappeared with these developments; Reform Street, South Inglis Street, East Queen Anne Street, Upper Station Road, James Place, Jigburn Terrace, Wooer's Alley, East Nethertown, South New Row, Market Street (since revived near to its original location) and Edgar Street (hopefully to be revived when the redevelopment of the Dunfermline and West Fife Hospital site is completed).

The railway system serving Dunfermline suffered in the 1960s as a result of the Beeching Report that recommended the closure of the Dunfermline–Alloa –Stirling line. This action resulted in there being no further need for the Upper Station or its goods and coal handling facility and when they closed so did the engine cleaning and maintenance unit to the north of Appin Crescent. It is perhaps ironic that there are plans being submitted for the reinstatement of goods traffic and subsequently passenger traffic from Stirling to Kincardine and, at a later date, Dunfermline.

The only plus point coming from the line to Stirling becoming redundant was that the low bridges in Halbeath Road, Townhill Road, Bruce Street and William Street could be dismantled and normal double-decker buses could be used throughout Dunfermline. Much of the track bed west and north of Dunfermline has been incorporated into the West Fife Millennium Cycleway. A side issue regarding the closure of rail lines was the unnecessary expense incurred by the Dunfermline Town Council in carrying out a scheme promoted by Provost Jean Mackie to provide a pedestrian tunnel under the railway north of Townhill. No sooner was the project completed than British Rail closed the line and demolished the bridge, thus making the tunnel redundant. A new railway station, Dunfermline–Queen Margaret, at Whitefield Road, opened in 2000.

The building of the Forth Road Bridge and its opening in September 1964 meant that Dunfermline was no longer isolated from Edinburgh and the south-east of Scotland and upgrading of the link from the bridge to the M8 and M9 in the next few years will make road travel to the west easier. It meant that the ferry service between North and South Queensferry, said to have been started by Queen Margaret 900 years before, was now redundant and the ferry boats were scrapped.

The subsequent building of the M90 until it eventually reached Perth also opened up access to the north and the East Fife regional road, built in 1983, from Halbeath to Glenrothes, gives ready access to east Fife and Dundee by means of the Tay Road Bridge. Provision was made in 1964 at the Pitreavie roundabout for an extension of the spur road to be built to form a Rosyth bypass and in 1987 plans for this were accepted, but some 16 years later they have yet to be acted upon.

The provision of port facilities at Rosyth that allowed the commencement of a vehicle and passenger ferry service between Rosyth and Zeebrugge in Belgium has opened up the prospect of more commercial and tourist traffic, not just passing through the area but also bringing great benefit to the town.

THE FORTH ROAD BRIDGE.
McEwan.
When the cables were completed, the work of building the supports for the roadway could begin. To maintain balance the work was carried out on both sides of the north and south towers simultaneously.

THE FORTH ROAD BRIDGE. *McEwan.*
This is the view from the top of the
south tower of the bridge looking
towards the Fife shore *c.*1962 when
the thousands of strands of wire that
would form the main suspension
cable were being spun across the
river.

FERRYTOLL JUNCTION. *D.C.L.*
Though named the Rosyth Labour Exchange it also served the people of Inverkeithing and was located at the junction of Castlelandhill Road and the road from Inverkeithing to North Queensferry. It was demolished *c.*1963 to allow the building of the approach road to the Forth Road Bridge.

PITREAVIE ROUNDABOUT. *D.C.L.*
Dunfermline was connected to the new M90 north of the Forth Road Bridge by a motorway spur from a new roundabout north of Rosyth. When this was built *c.*1963 provision was made for the road to be extended west on the proposed Rosyth bypass. 40 years later this is still eagerly awaited.

APPIN CRESCENT. *D.C.L.*
This area was known locally as the Park Gates. There was car parking and toilets for people using the tennis courts and the football pitches. The pub, shops and houses were demolished when the Sinclair Gardens roundabout was formed and a dangerous junction supposedly made safer.

HOLYROOD PLACE. *D.C.L.*
This view from the Park Gates looking towards the town centre shows Viewfield Baptist Church complete with the spire that was later removed for safety reasons, the rope works that became Gray's furniture store and St Margaret's Catholic Church. Behind the wall on the left of the *c.*1950 photograph is Benachie Lodge, which was demolished as part of the Sinclair Gardens road improvement scheme.

TOWNHILL ROAD. *D.C.L.*

This view taken in 1972 shows the last remaining property standing on the corner of Holyrood Place and Market Street with the new police station behind approaching completion. It would be officially opened in the following year. The low bridge that caught out drivers of high vehicles carries the railway line to the Upper Station. Benachie Lodge can be seen in the bottom right of the photograph which must have been taken around the Christmas period as one of the street decorations is hanging over the road junction.

MARKET STREET. *D.C.L.*

Children waiting to cross Market Street *c.*1960 when there was still a sweet shop on the corner of the street that gave access to the City and Royal Burgh of Dunfermline Cleansing Department and an Alexander's bus garage. The garage had been the depot for Simpson and Forrester who ran buses on the route to Leven via the coast and bus tours in the summer. The company was taken over by Alexander who retained the garage for buses that continued to serve the route from the Lower Bus Station. The street disappeared when the properties were demolished to allow the new police station to be built but the name was reused later for the road connecting James Street to Carnegie Drive.

MARKET STREET. *D.C.L.*
The cleansing department yard photographed *c.*1960 before the facility moved to a new purpose-built depot in Elgin Street.

DUNFERMLINE UPPER STATION. *D.C.L.*
The Upper Station closed after the rail line between Dunfermline, Alloa and Stirling was declared redundant under the Beeching proposals. As well as being a station for passenger traffic it was also the goods and coal depot for Dunfermline. There were also sidings that served the adjacent cattle market and Elder's grain mills. Hindsight makes it clear that if the station had been retained it could have formed an excellent interchange for rail travellers, giving access to the bus station, shopping centre, car park and city amenities.

UPPER STATION SITE. *D.C.L.*
The closure of the Upper Station made a large area of ground available for redevelopment. The photograph shows work being carried out in 1989 in preparation for the creation of the Carnegie Drive Retail Park.

DUNFERMLINE PUBLIC PARK. *D.P.G.*

The 1986 aerial photograph shows work being carried out on the new road, later to be named St Margaret's Drive, that would link Bothwell Gardens in the south with Sinclair Gardens in the north, thus diverting the increasing volume of traffic from the New Row, East Port and other routes through the city centre. The ground required for the building of the road could not be sold to Fife Regional Council because the Public Park belongs to the people of Dunfermline, and it was therefore exchanged for a piece of woodland that had formed part of the grounds of St Margaret's and Commercial schools.

NEW ROW. *D.C.L.*
In conjunction with the formation of St Margaret's Drive the New Row was blocked off and Woodmill Street rerouted to the south of the railway viaduct. The improvement to the junction meant that the Brig Tavern, shown here in the 1960s, would be demolished. An unsuccessful 'Save the Brig' campaign was run and a favourite watering hole was lost.

NEW ROW. *D.C.L.*
These houses and shops, here photographed in the 1960s, were demolished to allow the rerouting of Woodmill Street. Brucefield Avenue, beyond the railings, was blocked off.

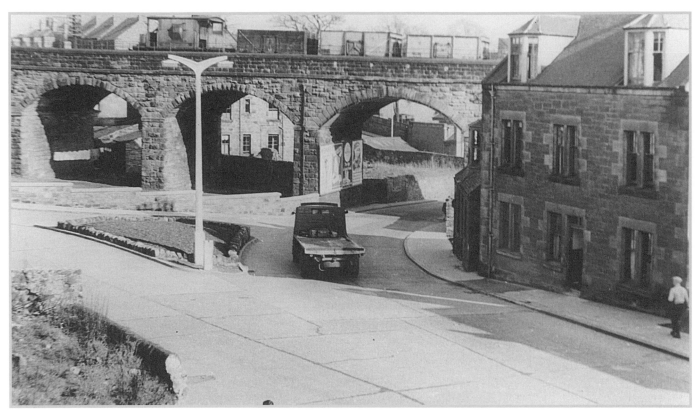

EAST NETHERTOWN BROAD STREET. *D.C.L.*
Prior to the demolition of the houses on the triangular piece of ground between Bothwell Street, New Row and East Nethertown the ground beneath the viaduct was the drying green used by the tenants. The 1970s photograph shows the washing hanging on the lines strung between hooks fastened to the stonework that are still there even though their users have long since moved away. There was still two-way traffic in Bothwell Street that made the New Row junction very dangerous.

NEW ROW JUNCTION. *D.C.L.*
This junction was known as 'the Gusset'. It was particularly dangerous because two-way traffic in the New Row met two-way traffic in Bothwell Street and vehicles exiting from Brucefield Avenue at this point. The properties were demolished to allow the formation of a roundabout, thus reducing accidents. The Dunfermline Co-operative Society owned the two shops shown in the 1970s photograph. The one on the corner was a baker's shop and the other in the New Row was a butcher's shop.

WOODMILL STREET. *D.C.L.*
These houses, photographed *c.*1950, were demolished and the street diverted to the south of the viaduct to make way for the new St Margaret's Drive.

ST LEONARD'S STREET. *D.C.L.*
The photograph, taken *c.*1970, shows the houses and shops on the west side of the street at the entrance to the bus garage. They were demolished to allow the street to be widened.

St Leonard's Street. *D.C.L.*

This block of flats opposite the entrance to the bus garage was demolished as part of the redevelopment of the area to allow access to the new supermarket that would be built a few years after this photograph was taken in the early 1970s. Another victim of the development would be St Leonard's Infant School, affectionately known as 'the Wee School', and which can be seen on the right. Mill Lane, which ran between these properties, led to Brucefield House and the boiler house of the adjacent Erskine Beveridge linen factory whose office block, seen beyond the school, was eventually converted into flat accommodation.

Hospital Hill. *McEwan.*

Hospital Hill at its junction with Izatt Avenue and St Andrew's Street in 1999 when the road was being made into a dual carriageway.

CARNEGIE STREET. *D.C.L. (M.A.)*

Until the new bus station between James Street and Carnegie Drive was built all bus services serving routes to the north, east and west of Dunfermline left from the 'Top' or Upper Bus Station, west of the fire station in Carnegie Street shown on this photograph taken in 1959. The various stances were covered but otherwise open to the wind and rain that blew through them. Facilities provided on the site were an office and waiting room, toilets, Drummond's Snack Bar and a 'phone box. The move to the new bus station did not provide much more comfort as waiting passengers were still given little shelter from the prevailing wind and rain.

UPPER BUS STATION. *George Robertson.*

Stance Number 1 from which buses on the route to Ballingry left. The photograph taken *c.*1960 shows one of the Guy double-decker buses on that route. In the early 1950s they had wooden slatted instead of upholstered seats that were more easily cleaned after miners or factory workers had used them. At that time the queue for the service between 5 and 6 o'clock could be 200yds long, with buses leaving as soon as they were full of factory workers going home to Crossgates, Cowdenbeath, Lochgelly and Ballingry. The service to Kelty left from the adjacent stance.

UPPER BUS STATION. *D.C.L. (E.M.C.)*
This wooden hut served as waiting room, parcel office, booking office and bus station superintendent's office for the life of the bus station. The posters and advertisements show the destinations of bus tours departing from Dunfermline *c.*1950.

MOODIE STREET. *D.C.L.*
The view looking up Moodie Street in 1958 from its junction with Rolland Street, before the road improvements which meant that a road was created through the small park, known locally as 'the Daisy Park', adjacent to the Andrew Carnegie Birthplace. The properties on the left of the street were demolished and the area landscaped.

MOODIE STREET. *D.C.L.*
The junction of Moodie Street in 1958 before the properties were demolished and the road diverted to the east to improve the junction. This section of road was exchanged for the part of the adjacent park that was required for the road alterations and now belongs to the Carnegie Dunfermline Trust and provides access and parking for the Andrew Carnegie Birthplace and Memorial Hall.

PRIORY LANE. *D.P.G.*
These properties were being demolished in 1964 to allow the remaining portion of Priory Lane to be widened. Widening had started at the New Row end almost 75 years previously.

PRIORY LANE, NEW
ROW JUNCTION.
D.C.L.
The junction of
Priory Lane with the
New Row required
improvement after
the realignment at
the other end of the
street had been
completed and the
properties shown
here in the late 1960s
were demolished.
Massive buttresses
had to be built to
support the gable
wall of the adjoining
Pub and Guesthouse.

JAMES STREET. *D.C.L. (E.M.C.)*
The building of the multi-storey car park and bus station meant that these properties would disappear between 1979 and 1982. The first property on the left was the garage of John Scott, butcher. Next was Philip's garage, later used as Bernard's taxi office and garage. The two-storey house was the office of Hoggan and Sons, painters, followed by a single-storey house that at one time was the home of Mr Foggo who was manager of the City Bakery and scoutmaster of the 2nd Fife YMCA Scout Troup. The large ventilator on the rear of the cinema can be seen on the right.

JAMES STREET. *D.C.L.*
The properties on the left of the photograph taken *c*.1977 were all destined to be demolished for the Kingsgate development. The steps led to the James Street Gospel Hall. The property on the right is still in use.

INGLIS STREET. *D.C.L.*
By the time that this photograph was taken in 1981 the properties on the right of the street had been demolished and the area, together with what had been the Dunfermline Cattle Market, turned into car parking. The British Rail posters show the start of the footpath that led to the Upper Station and immediately next to that was the entrance to the market and on many occasions cattle would escape and be chased by their handlers along Reform Street. Beyond the railway bridge is the entrance to the rail goods yard, at the north end of which was the office of coal merchant George Adamson. Elder's City Mills are in the background.

PILMUIR STREET. *George Robertson.*
This part of Pilmuir Street was originally called Bath Street because the baths which Andrew Carnegie had gifted to Dunfermline were there. The public house on the corner was called the Bath Tavern for the same logical reason, and is now Coady's for no apparent reason. The bus, photographed *c.*1971 outside Pilmuir Hall, the former baths, is on the local service to Beatty Place.

INGLIS STREET. *George Robertson.*
This bus stop in Inglis Street was where most passengers coming to Dunfermline in the early 1960s from Kelty, Kirkcaldy or Cowdenbeath alighted as it was the nearest point to the shops.

WOODMILL ROAD. *D.C.L.*
In 1964 Woodmill Road was a fairly quiet lane with the entrance to the Transy Estate on the left and Ferguson's rose fields on the right.

WOODMILL ROAD. *D.P.G.*
The development of part of the Transy Estate as the site for the new St Margaret's and Commercial Primary School meant that, later in 1964, the road was widened. A strip of ground was acquired from Ferguson and eventually the whole of the former nursery was developed as a housing estate.

ROSYTH RAILWAY STATION. *D.C.L.*
A railway station was built to serve the new Garden City of Rosyth in 1917. It had the status of a halt rather than full station status and only had small shelters for travellers.

ROSYTH RAILWAY STATION. *D.C.L. (E.M.C.)*
The ticket office for Rosyth Halt was built in a position where it could serve both platforms and was well known to service personnel and their families travelling from all over Britain to Rosyth. The office closed in 1994 and was then used by the Forthview Community Housing Association before it was finally demolished.

ROSYTH CROSSROADS. *D.C.L.*

This photograph of the Rosyth Crossroads is dated 1951 but that must be wrong as the graffiti showing E II R could not have been written before the Queen ascended the throne in 1952. Individuals who contested the title, since an Elizabeth had never ruled Scotland until now, painted these comments on sites throughout Scotland. Some people took this further by planting bombs in pillarboxes. This led to the removal of the royal cipher from all mail vans and pillarboxes in Scotland. The Crossroads roundabout has undergone many changes in an attempt to reduce the number of accidents that occur there. The surrounding buildings including the kiosk remain unchanged.

ROAD TRANSPORT. *D.C.L.*

The photograph shows the vehicles and staff of David West and Son at the Rumblingwell premises of the firm on the day before nationalisation took effect in 1949. When the firm was nationalised David West, on the right of the photograph, was employed as BRS regional manager and his son James, on the left, as depot manager. The firm was later privatised, renationalised and finally once more privatised.

PITTENCRIEFF STREET. *D.C.L.*

The crossroads of Pittencrieff Street, William Street and Coal Road, photographed *c.*1960, was the location of many accidents. Eventually all of the properties except the three-storey block of houses were demolished and traffic lights were erected to further improve the junction. The work was to be part of a scheme to make Pittencrieff Street into a dual carriageway but this project has been dropped within the past few years.

DUNFERMLINE LOWER STATION. *D.C.L. (E.M.C.)*

The photograph dated *c.*1950 shows Dunfermline Lower Station in the days when it had three platforms, which all had canopies over them. There were machines that sold chocolate and chewing gum and another machine that embossed aluminium strips to be used as name labels. The platforms were long enough to accommodate the long Aberdeen to London trains. The name was recently changed to Dunfermline Town. Attempts to have it renamed Dunfermline City have so far been unsuccessful.

INDUSTRY

Industrial and commercial development was slow to get moving after the war. Most of the major employers were established in premises that were large enough for their immediate needs. This remained the position until the devastating decline in the basic industries of linen, silk and coal. Most of the factories closed and were adapted for other commercial purposes by being subdivided into small manufacturing, storage or retail units. The regeneration of manufacturing in Dunfermline began in 1961 when the Monotype Corporation built a new factory in Halbeath Road that was twice extended and remained in production until 1982. Lyle and Scott also opened a factory in 1961 at Primrose Lane, Rosyth, to manufacture underwear. This factory closed c.1992. Phillips established a factory in 1971 at Queensferry Road to manufacture electronic equipment. This factory was later sold to Solectron and has been extended on a number of occasions. The building of this factory led to the establishment of the Pitreavie Industrial Estate in 1973. An early tenant on the estate was the Dunfermline Press Group who moved there from their printing establishment in New Row.

A whisky blending and bottling plant was built on the Pitreavie estate by Arthur Bell and it remained in production until 1992 when it was closed and sold to become a distribution centre for KwikSave who were subsequently taken over by Somerfield. The Bank of Scotland established their Visa Centre on the estate in 1985. In 1994 the Dunfermline Building Society moved their headquarters building from East Port to new premises on the east side of Queensferry Road and this initiated the creation of the Carnegie Campus which has expanded on to land previously owned by the Ministry of Defence at Pitreavie Castle. A call centre for Sky opened on the south side of the castle in 1995 and Lexmark opened a factory at Admiralty Road in 1996. Other smaller industrial estates were formed at Dickson Street, Halbeath Drive and Primrose Lane.

The largest development in the history of Dunfermline was the commencement of the building of a manufacturing complex for the Hyundai Corporation to the east of the town and which would form the basis of the industrial development in the eastern expansion plans. Building was started in 1997 but before the work was completed, occupation of the factory was put on hold because of uncertainties in the electronics market. The factory was never fitted out and Hyundai sold the building to Motorola, who have yet to declare, due to the continuing uncertainty, if and when production will start there.

In 1984 the vast petro-chemical complex at Mossmorran near Cowdenbeath together with the new tanker terminal at Braefoot Bay near Aberdour was inaugurated. Unfortunately the associated manufacturing industries that should have followed and produced a great many job opportunities never materialised.

The naval dockyard and repair yard at Rosyth together with coal mining had been the major employers in the Dunfermline area for many years. Coal mining declined rapidly after the war until all of the pits in the area closed. The building of Longannet power station produced a fight back when a complex of mines was opened to supply it with coal. The complex closed in 2002 and with it coal mining in west Fife ceased. There are still a number of opencast mining sites around Dunfermline. The decline in the defence requirement after the war saw the naval dockyard under constant threat of closure. The need for a refitting base for Trident submarines was thought to be the saviour for the yard and work began on a new dock in readiness for what was thought an almost automatic awarding of the contract to Rosyth. Devonport won the contract and Rosyth was left with a very large hole in the ground. Privatisation of the naval repair yards saw management being taken over by Babcock and the yard has been very successful in obtaining refitting contracts for many ships of the Royal Navy. It is hoped that it will also be involved in the building of the new class of super aircraft carriers. The departure of the Royal Navy with the removal of the minesweeper squadron from the dockyard meant that there was now a vast area of surplus ground available for redevelopment.

Offices, industrial estates and storage units have been built or existing buildings adapted. Hotels and leisure facilities are planned which, together with the new ferry handling facility, look like establishing Rosyth Port as a major employer once more.

The formation of many smaller companies means that in times of recession the likelihood of thousands of workers being faced with redundancy is considerably lessened.

DUNFERMLINE SILK MILLS. *D.C.L. (M.A.)*
Dunfermline Silk Mills had manufacturing facilities and office premises in St Leonard's Works. It was one of three factories in Dunfermline weaving silk. The photograph was taken in the inspection department in the 1950s.

ST LEONARD'S WORKS. *D.C.L. (M.A.)*
Erskine Beveridge St Leonard's Linen Works was a major producer of linen products in Dunfermline. Mrs Wildridge is seen in the 1957 photograph working at the machine that produced the punched cards that controlled the jacquard looms that wove intricate patterns in the linen.

St Leonard's Works, Lap Room. *D.C.L.*
Nettie Weir, shown on this photograph taken *c.*1950, was in charge of the lap room at the St Leonard's Linen Works. The lap room was where the finished cloth was cut and folded.

Winterthur Silk Factory. *D.C.L.*
The photograph is titled 'The Staff of Winterthur Silk Factory, Bruce Street, *c.*1965' but may only include heads of departments with Mr Bosshart in the centre of the front row. This was the factory that wove silk material for the future Queen Elizabeth's wedding dress in 1947.

LYLE AND SCOTT FACTORY. *D.C.L. (E.M.C.)*
A purpose-built factory for the production of knitted cotton goods was erected at Primrose Lane, Rosyth, for Lyle and Scott. When the factory closed it was converted into a bowling alley and expansion to house further leisure activities was planned but never happened. After a fire the premises closed.

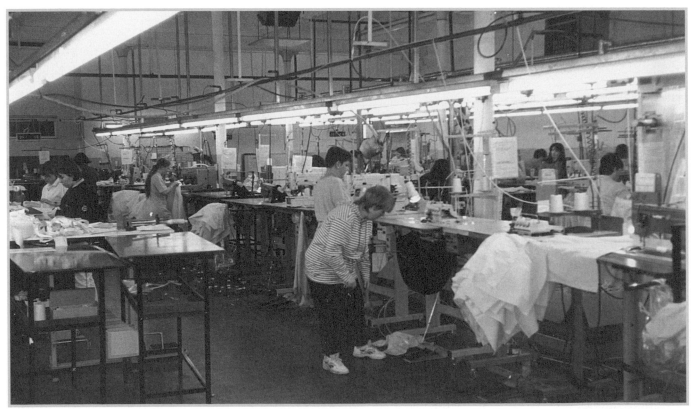

CASTLEBLAIR LIMITED. *D.C.L. (Andy Lawrence)*
The company originated in the former premises of the Castleblair Silk Mills and soon expanded to include Victoria Works and St Margaret's Works. They produce and market a wide range of clothing. The photograph is taken in the department known as the Back Flat in 1997.

BALDRIDGE WORKS. *D.C.L.*

There were a large number of manufacturers of aerated waters, lemonade and soft drinks in Dunfermline due to the purity of the water supply from the wells where the factories were originally established. Mitchell had a factory in Carnegie Street and the Woodrow factory was in Rolland Street before transferring to the Pitreavie Business Park. Gilbert Rae owned Baldridge Works, located at the corner of William Street and Golfdrum Street.

BISSET'S WORKS. *D.C.L.*

Some of the lemonade factories also bottled beer and cider, and Bisset in Pittencrieff Street operated one such bottling plant. The photograph shows one of the company vehicles decorated for display, probably at Civic Week *c*.1950.

DUNFERMLINE CO-OPERATIVE CREAMERY. *D.C.L.*
The Co-operative Creamery was located at Grantsbank, off Pilmuir Street, and dairy products were distributed from there to the various Society branches and to customers' doorsteps. Some of the Creamery staff are shown on the photograph that was taken *c*.1960. Alex Allan on the left was chauffeur to the society secretary, Philip Douglas.

UCSB BAKERY. *D.C.L.*
A bakery was built off Limekilns Road by the United Co-operative Society to serve the east of Scotland but the project was short lived. The photograph is of an official visit *c*.1950. After the demolition of the bakery the land was developed as Liggars Place housing estate.

CITY BAKERY. *D.C.L. (E.M.C.)*
Dunfermline City Bakeries Ltd had shops in Queen Anne Street and in High Street. The Bakery linked the premises. The photograph shows the access lane for deliveries. The building on the right of the photograph taken in 1978 was an electricity sub-station and behind that was the office used by the installation inspectors of the south of Scotland Electricity Board.

MINERS' STRIKE MARCH. *D.P.G.*
The miners' strike in 1972 was for better wages and Adam Hunter, MP and a youthful Les Wood led a march through the streets of Dunfermline.

HMS *Caledonia*. D.C.L. (M.A.)

HMS *Caledonia* was attached to the Rosyth naval base and was the training establishment for naval artificers. The 1955 photograph shows the parade for the unveiling of the figurehead at the gate of the establishment.

HMS *Cochrane*. D.C.L. (Martin Rogers)

The shore base for the Royal Navy dockyard at Rosyth was HMS *Cochrane*. It was initially built as an administration and accommodation establishment for WRNS during World War Two but changed post-war to its shore base role.

FRASER AND CARMICHAEL. *D.C.L.*

This warehouse was the office and distribution facility for Fraser and Carmichael who distributed groceries to shops, hotels and businesses throughout Scotland. The company also owned the City Hotel, shops in Dunfermline and the surrounding district and Maclay's Brewery in Alloa. They held the concession for the importation of lentils to Scotland and one of their biggest selling items at one time was tallow for miners' lamps. The photograph was taken shortly after the firm ceased trading in 1971 and the premises were demolished two years later allowing visitors an uninterrupted view of Dunfermline Abbey. The sign for the police office can be seen on the right. In 1971 it was in part of the City Chambers and had cells below. Its entrance was opposite the end of Maygate.

PRESS OFFICE. *D.C.L.*

Two identical buildings flanked the entrance to Canmore School in the New Row. The north building, which still exists in its original state, was the Wilson Institute. The south building housed the offices and printing works of the Dunfermline Press until they moved to the Pitreavie Business Park in 1975. The photograph shows the frontage of the building being removed to allow a modern office to be constructed in 1950. The work took four years to complete.

PREMISES OF JAMES WILSON & CO. *D.C.L.*
Wilson the Printers, as they were more commonly known, operated in premises that formerly housed the printing press of the *West Fife Journal* until they were transferred to Bruce Street. Wilsons carried out commercial printing and sold office furniture and stationery. The photograph taken *c.*1966 shows the typical 1960s shop front.

ELDER & CO. *D.C.L. (M.A.)*
This is the staff of Hugh Elder & Co. *c.*1960. The grain mill on its site at the corner of Inglis Street and Campbell Street dominated the skyline. The building had its own railway siding served by a line from the adjacent Upper Station.

THE DUNFERMLINE GOLF FACTORY. *D.C.L.*
The staff of the St Andrews Golf Factory are embarking on an outing in 1946 to St Andrew's for the first Open Golf Championship to be held after World War Two. The championship was won by Sam Snead. The company was seldom given its correct title and was more commonly known as the Dunfermline Golf Factory.

MCFARLANE'S SCRAP YARD, PITTENCRIEFF STREET. *D.C.L.*
This was not just a scrap yard, it was an industry. As well as a recovery service for crashed vehicles, Willie McFarlane bought Rolls-Royce cars that he prepared for export to the US. He also had an interest in steam engines and his yard was home to a number of road rollers. For many years he thwarted Council plans to improve the area by refusing to be relocated or to close his premises, but he was finally forced to admit defeat when overtaken by plans to redevelop Pittencrieff Street were approved.

LOCHSIDE FIRECLAY AND BRICK WORKS. *D.C.L.*
Townhill Brickworks manufactured bricks and a large range of fireclay products from toilets to statues and garden furniture. The young boys on the photograph that is dated *c.*1961 are inspecting a kiln that is being used to make chimney liners. The company became part of the Hepworth Organisation and manufactured pipes for their 'Hepseal' range of products until its closure.

STAFF OF **J.D. & W. HAMILTON.** *McEwan.*

After the war many returning servicemen started small businesses. One electrical contractors business started then was J.D. & W. Hamilton, who had workshop premises and later showrooms in Chapel Street. Five of the electrical staff, Willie Anderson, Wilson Ferguson, the author, Tom Gallacher and Henry Aspey are photographed *c.*1950 in front of one of the company's vehicles.

GEORGE KAY & SONS. *D.C.L.*

Kay's Panel Beaters and Coach Builders in Inglis Street was where many Dunfermline drivers ended after having major or minor accidents with their vehicles. Jackson in Pittencrieff Street and McIvor in Mill Street offered similar services. With the development of the area in 1983 to allow the building of the multi-storey car park and bus station, Kay's was relocated in Campbell Street.

HOUSING

Dunfermline in 1945 was considerably smaller than today. The only housing development that took place during the war years was the building of houses for essential dockyard workers in the area bounded by Beveridge Street and Wedderburn Street. Another development in Rosyth at that time was nicknamed 'Dollytown' because the houses were so small.

There was no need for the large-scale rebuild of war-damaged properties in Dunfermline after the war. Houses had been damaged and destroyed in Kingseat, unfortunately resulting in a fatality, several bombs fell near the present junction of Woodmill Road and Linburn Road and there was a severe firebomb attack on an empty field behind the McKane playing fields, but Dunfermline neither suffered nor benefited from enemy action. The need for house building was a social need. Houses were required for homecoming troops and as an urgent replacement for the many houses that lacked the basic elements for post-war living.

With the exception of council and private houses that had been built in the immediate pre-war period, most houses in Dunfermline had only town gas for heating, lighting and cooking. The post-war decade saw the installation of electricity for these purposes resulting in such an increase in demand for power that additional gas-turbine generators were installed at Townhill Power Station in order to meet the demand at peak periods.

With the introduction of electricity for cooking, housewives no longer had to endure the miseries of the dreaded kitchen range. No more buffing and black-leading and no more lighting of a fire before breakfast could be cooked. Ranges were ripped out and shining 'easy clean' tiled fireplaces were installed. Modern living had arrived.

The next logical progression was the purchase of a washing machine. This meant an end to early rising to light the washhouse boiler, and the power wringer and electric iron saw the demise of the mangle. Indeed many outside washhouses were now only used for storage and the old wooden tubs were converted to plant tubs.

Provision of new housing began with the building of prefabs at Elliot Street, Malcolm Street, Beck

PREFABS. *D.C.L. (M.A.)*
Two types of prefabs (prefabricated houses) were built in the Dunfermline area. Within Dunfermline most were aluminium but in the surrounding district many were corrugated asbestos. They were extremely popular and had bathrooms and fitted kitchens. While built as temporary housing, they existed until the 1960s. The 1956 photograph shows one of a number of prefabs in Townhill.

Crescent, Rosyth, Kingseat and Townhill. These houses were bungalows that were delivered in sections or in kit form, quickly erected on prepared foundations, connected to electricity and water supplies and sewage systems, and were ready for occupation in a few days.

The bungalows boasted fitted kitchens and bathrooms and were easily heated and maintained. They were the pride and joy of many families who were sad to see them demolished in the late 1960s. The so-called temporary houses had endured for over 20 years. Another 'quick build' solution to the need for housing was the Swedish Timber house. A number of these were built at Blair Drive and are still going strong.

The urgent need to replace the condemned substandard properties throughout the town was tackled in 1947 when the housing schemes at Izatt Avenue and at Burnside Street in Rosyth were commenced. The growth of coal mining in the area saw an influx of miners from the west of Scotland and this led to non-traditional steel houses being built at Woodmill in 1947.

Until 1948 James Shearer, a local architect, advised the Town Council on planning matters but the task was becoming onerous. It was decided that a new post of town planning officer should be created and Miss Annie Turnbull was appointed at a salary of £750 per annum. The following year, on her advice, the Town Council decided that the solution to the housing waiting list was to purchase 240 acres of land at Aberdour Road in order to build the largest housing estate in Dunfermline. The Abbeyview housing estate, where building continued for 20 years, is Miss Turnbull's legacy. While the scheme looks good on a street map, no consideration had been given to the contours of the area and this resulted in shops and community facilities being built on the top of the hill and steeply terraced streets running down into the

JIGBURN TERRACE. *D.P.G.*

Jigburn Terrace, or the Jig as it was more commonly known, was north of Baldridgeburn and consisted of blocks of tenement houses with outside toilets, coal cellars and washhouses. The Rintoul family, who also owned one of the model lodging houses in Chapel Street, and who were constantly at war with the Town Council, owned the property. The property and its occupant frequently achieved doubtful notoriety. It was finally demolished in 1962 but as can be seen by the photograph, the Jigburn Store remained open until the last tenant was flitted out.

valleys on either side. Nevertheless it was a popular housing area and offered a degree of luxury to people who had been used to outside and shared toilets, no baths, no hot water and no central heating, and a community spirit soon developed. It is only in recent years that some of the blocks of flats have become unpopular with tenants leading to many being demolished and sections of the scheme being included in a Regeneration Plan.

The beginning of the 'swinging 60s' saw the building of the only three high-rise blocks of flats in Dunfermline at Broomhead Drive in 1961. In the late 1960s council housing expanded further with the building of 500 houses on the area between Garvock Hill and Woodmill Road and a further development of 87 houses between the Abbeyview scheme and Aberdour Road.

New housing was built in Rosyth north and south of Primrose Lane in 1968 and 1976. By 1980 building land for council housing was at a premium and the Council decided to redevelop an area bounded by Moodie Street, Reid Street, Rolland Street and Nethertown Broad Street. They then concentrated on the provision of high amenity and sheltered housing at Bellyeoman, Baldridgeburn and Keir Hardie Terrace.

The villages of Wellwood and Kingseat were redeveloped with the demolition of the old miners' rows and the building of replacement modern housing in 1952 and 1962 respectively. Council house building ceased in 1993 due to the recently introduced government 'right to buy' policy.

Private housing schemes sprang up in the early 1960s with the areas between Garvock Hill and Halbeath Road being developed and at the end of the decade the land to the south of Garvock Hill was also taken over.

Wimpey purchased West Pitcorthie Farm from Mr Harley and building started there in the late 1960s. The Wimpey scheme can be recognised by the nearly all of the streets being named after trees or shrubs. Other contractors developed the area north to Aberdour Road.

By 1982 the population of Dunfermline was 60,000 having risen from a pre-war figure of around 40,000. A report commissioned in 1946 by the Carnegie Dunfermline Trust on the 'Future Development of Dunfermline' by James Shearer envisaged a maximum population of 50,000–60,000.

Private house builders obtained planning permission for the development of East Baldridge Farm to the north-west of the town in 1984.

The growth in population and the apparent insatiable demand for housing resulted in further developments between 1992 and 1996 with development of the fields to the north and east of the new Queen Margaret Hospital in the Whitefield Road area.

It became obvious that the existing boundaries of the City and Royal Burgh of Dunfermline were limiting future expansion and after protracted and frequently bitter arguments between the local authorities and potential developers as to whether the future expansion should be to the east or west of the town, it was decided that a major expansion of Dunfermline would be planned on the land between Linburn Road and the M90 motorway. The development would consist of housing, including 'affordable' housing, industrial, commercial and recreational facilities with sufficient land for a 20-year timescale.

The current demand for housing by people who work in Edinburgh and further afield, but who find that it is cheaper to live in Dunfermline and commute, and the pace at which the developers are building to meet that demand, makes it likely that the land available for housing will be filled before that date. Unfortunately the building of the other elements of the project is not yet, in 2004, being carried out.

ALBANY STREET. *D.C.L. (E.M.C.)*
The tenements on the north side of Albany Street were demolished in the late 1950s as part of a slum clearance scheme by the Town Council and many of the tenants were rehoused in the Trondheim Parkway area of the Abbeyview housing scheme. After the houses were vacated vandals and arsonists targeted them.

BOTHWELL STREET. *D.C.L.*
This tenement block photographed *c*.1970 housed more than 36 families and was demolished to allow the street to be widened. The Bank of Scotland now occupies part of the site.

DOLLYTOWN, ROSYTH. *D.C.L.*
These houses, built on the east side of Castle Road shortly after the war started, were small and compact and soon the area gained the nickname Dollytown. This is often confused with Tin Town which was the village of houses built for the workers and their families who were employed in the construction of the dockyard and which were demolished when the houses of the Rosyth Garden City were built in the 1920s.

EDGAR STREET. *D.C.L.*
Edgar Street was a short street from Reid Street to the gates of Priory House, the mansion that was the Nurses' Home of the Dunfermline and West Fife Hospital. The street ceased to exist when its tenement blocks and small cottages were demolished to make way for the new Casualty Department of the Hospital that opened in 1958, eight years after this photograph was taken. The parents of Andrew Carnegie lived in Edgar Street for a number of years. The communal drying greens and gardens that lay between Reid Street and Edgar Street were the happy playground of the many children who lived in the area. The street name is to be revived and used in the housing development that will take the place of the old hospital.

GOLFDRUM STREET. *D.C.L.*
Nearly all of the houses in Golfdrum Street were demolished and new blocks of flats, terraced houses and a home for the elderly erected. This road junction at the west end of the street was improved.

GOLFDRUM STREET. *D.C.L.*
A number of the old cottages in Golfdrum Street had been weavers' cottages. A weaver who lived in one of them wanted to make the treadle hole under his loom deeper and was hammering at a stone that blocked his progress. He soon stopped when an old neighbour told him that it was the capping stone of one of the many mineshafts in the area, and breaking through it would deposit him at the bottom of the shaft.

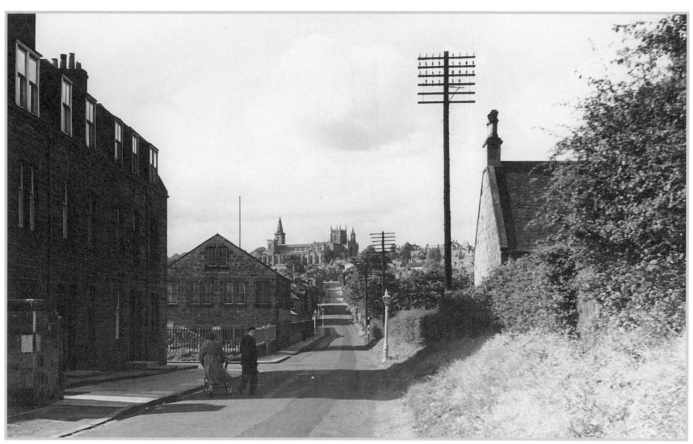

ELGIN STREET. *D.C.L. (E. Wallace)*
Now the site of an industrial estate, Dickson Street and the south end of Elgin Street were where many of the workers in the adjacent Stewart's Rubber Works lived. By the time this 1986 photograph was taken the works had been closed and converted into premises for small businesses. The houses were demolished as part of a slum clearance scheme and the community dispersed to different areas of Dunfermline.

WEDDERBURN STREET. *D.C.L.*
The photograph shows the Wedderburn Street/Blacklaw Road junction in 1952 when the new housing development at Abbeyview was started.

WOODMILL HOUSING. *D.C.L. (Cunningham)*
A small housing development was built in 1949 at the junction of Blacklaw Road and Woodmill Road. The houses were erected by Weir and had steel outer shells. They were built to house miners moving in to the area from the west of Scotland to work in the Fife coal pits. Like the prefabs before them they were designed to have a short life but roughcasting them and installing new heating systems later extended this.

IZATT AVENUE. *D.C.L.*
The housing estate to the south of the Dunfermline High School was started immediately after the war with the roads which would become Izatt Avenue, Jennie Rennie's Road and Shearer Square being laid out for the building of terraced houses, each with their own front and back gardens.

ABBEYVIEW HOUSING ESTATE. *D.C.L.*

The aerial photograph of the Abbeyview Housing Estate *c*.1965 shows the initial phase of house building complete. Future development would take place south to Aberdour Road with the Scottish Special Housing Association development, north of Woodmill Road with the Touch development that would include a school, church, shopping and community facilities. Private housing would be built on the south side of Garvock Hill and in the fields south of Woodmill Road on the site of Ferguson's rose fields. St Margaret's and Commercial Primary Schools would be built in the grounds of the Transy Estate and St Columba's High School at the junction of Woodmill Road and Linburn Road.

BUTE CRESCENT. *D.C.L.*

In the northern area of Abbeyview the streets were named after Scottish islands and in the southern area they were named after Scottish rivers and hills. Both areas had streets named after Provosts of Dunfermline. The Co-operative baker with his horse and cart is here seen *c*.1960 selling his wares in Bute Crescent. Those were the days when children could still be sent out alone to make purchases and when the balconies of the flats had yet to become additional storage areas. The horse has left a bonus for any keen gardener in the area.

BROOMHEAD PARK. *D.C.L. (M.A.)*
This area would soon become the site of the only high-rise development in Dunfermline. The park was a venue for the Dunfermline and West Fife Agricultural Show and to the south was a large area of garden allotments. The new Queen Anne School is on the right of the photograph that was taken *c.*1959. The fields of East Baldridge farm that will eventually be used for a private housing development are at the top of the photograph.

BROOMHEAD MULTI-STOREY DEVELOPMENT. *D.C.L.*
The photograph, *c.*1960, shows the building of one of the three high-rise blocks of flats at Broomhead Park. When they were built they were the height of modernity with electric under-floor heating, lifts and rubbish chutes. No more climbing upstairs with shopping and carrying rubbish downstairs. The special concrete mix used in the construction was designed to keep water out but it also kept condensation in. Because the tenants found the electric heating to be costly, they kept the windows of the flats closed and this resulted in worsening condensation problems. This, together with security problems, vandalism and fires being lit in the rubbish chutes, meant the flats became less popular.

Broomhead Flats. *D.C.L. (M.A.)*
A proud tenant with her family and dog enjoys the view from their vantage point high above Dunfermline shortly after Provost Jean Mackie carried out the official opening ceremony and the first tenants moved into their houses in 1961.

Trenchard Place. *D.C.L.*
Following the demolition of Jigburn Terrace and the surrounding buildings, a small development of housing for the elderly was built.

BELLYEOMAN FARM. *D.C.L.*
The photograph was taken in 1958 from the top of the chimney at Hill's Laundry in Halbeath Road. It looks over Milldean Grove to the fields of Bellyeoman Farm that would become the site of the new general hospital for Dunfermline. The remainder of the area would be used for a housing estate with shops, school, nursing home, sheltered housing, church and doctors' surgery.

GARVOCKHILL. *D.C.L.*
Preparatory work being carried out in 1959 with the laying of drains before the new roads, Thimblehall Drive and Gowanbrae Drive, would be formed and houses built on the fields between Garvockhill and Halbeath Road.

SPORT

Mention sport and the first, and possibly the only one to spring to mind for some, would be football. Dunfermline Athletic Football Team, the Pars, has played in most of the Scottish football leagues over the past 60 years. The team's greatest achievements were no doubt when in 1961 and 1968 they won the Scottish Cup. These wins gave them entry into European football competitions in which they gave as good as they got and earned Dunfermline Athletic a reputation for competitive football in England and throughout Europe. The money which was earned by the club at that time allowed the building of a new stand which led to further ground improvements and the provision of seated accommodation for all of the supporters in accordance with modern safety requirements. Amateur football is played at various grounds in and around Dunfermline.

Dunfermline is well served with excellent golf courses. Canmore to the north of the town and Pitreavie to the south are both long-established courses. Dunfermline Golf Club moved to Pitfirrane estate, Crossford, from Torryburn in 1953 when their old course was threatened by mining and a proposed road development. The estate was purchased by the Carnegie Dunfermline Trust and rented to the club to provide it with a new home and the club purchased the estate from the Trust for £12,000 in 1966. If the club ever sells the estate they will be required to pay a further £16,000. A new golf course was opened at Forrester Park, Cairneyhill, in 2002.

Bowling has been a pastime in Dunfermline since at least the 16th century when it was played by James VI in the grounds of Dunfermline monastery. The public probably did not get a game until 1852 when the Dunfermline Bowling Club was formed. This club, which plays at its green in Priory Lane, was joined by others over the years including Dunfermline Northern, West End, Townhill Kingseat, Nethertown, Headwell, Rosyth and Abbeyview. With the exception of the Dunfermline club, the Carnegie Dunfermline Trust, a private landowner or Fife Council owns the greens on which the club members play. Headwell Bowling Club opened an indoor rink in 2003.

The Carnegie Dunfermline Trust created the Pitreavie sports ground on land south of Dunfermline to provide pitches for football, hockey and cricket. A sports pavilion, built there in 1933, was formally opened by Mrs Louise Carnegie the following year. When built the pavilion had a large central clock tower but this was removed in around 1949. A running track was added in 1954 with a grandstand being built six years later.

A clubhouse was sponsored by Babcock Rosyth Defence Ltd and opened in 1997. In 1963 the area was handed over to Dunfermline Town Council and in 2001 Fife council entered into an agreement with Vida to manage and rejuvenate the complex. New five-a-side and full-size all-weather football pitches were constructed and formally opened in 2003 and there are plans for an indoor practice running track. Cricket is also played at McKane Park, which is also the home of Dunfermline Rugby Club and Squash Club.

The Carnegie Centre in Pilmuir Street has facilities for competitive and leisure swimming, Turkish baths, gymnasium, fitness centre, squash courts and a large sports hall. Many of the high schools are now community schools offering sports facilities to the public outwith school hours.

While many public tennis courts have closed or converted to other purposes due to lack of funding and lack of use, there is a very active Dunfermline Lawn Tennis and Bridge Club whose courts and clubhouse are located in Bothwell Street. The leisure complex at Halbeath includes a fitness club and the Keavil hotel in Crossford also has similar facilities.

Sailing and similar pursuits can be fulfilled a short distance from the town at various riverside locations on the Forth.

DUNFERMLINE ATHLETIC BRING HOME THE CUP, 1961. *D.P.G.*

In 1961 Dunfermline Athletic beat Celtic at Hamden Park in the Scottish Cup Final. They won the replay having drawn the match on the previous Saturday. When the team returned to Dunfermline they were mobbed by fans as they paraded the cup through the streets of the town on an open top bus.

DUNFERMLINE FANS QUEUE FOR TICKETS AT EAST END PARK, 1961. *D.P.G.*

Some people queued for six hours to get a ticket for the appearance of Dunfermline Athletic in the Scottish Cup Final.

JOCK STEIN AND A TEAM OF CELEBRITIES, 1964. *D.C.L. (M.A.)*
Frequently charity football and cricket matches were held between celebrity teams during Civic Week.

PEGASUS AFC DOCKYARD APPRENTICES FOOTBALL TEAM, 1964–5. *D.C.L.*
There are many amateur football clubs that play on a regular basis in and around Dunfermline. This team won the Rosyth Mid-day League in the 1964–5 season.

DUNFERMLINE CRICKET TEAM, 1960. *D.P.G.*

The team are photographed in front of the old stand at McKane Park. The Cricket and Rugby Clubs shared the ground at McKane Park for many years until an additional adjacent piece of ground became available allowing a rugby pitch to be laid out. The clubhouse was modernised and a squash court built.

CARNEGIE SWIMMING CLUB, YOUNG PRIZEWINNERS, 1973. *D.P.G.*

Over the many years of its existence the Carnegie Swimming Club has produced top-class swimmers who have gone on to win national and international Awards. Perhaps some of these young prizewinners also did that.

ATHLETICS MATCH AT PITREAVIE RUNNING TRACK, **1962.** *D.C.L. (N)*

To celebrate American Independence Day a match was held at the Pitreavie running track between the SAAA and Atlanta on 4 July 1962. No sophisticated photo-finish equipment was used, just a ribbon from the box on the right-hand post held by a junior official at the other side of the track. The bell rung to indicate the last lap can be seen at the bottom of the post, again nothing fancy, only an old school hand bell. The match would appear to have been well attended.

DUNFERMLINE RUGBY CLUB, **1951.** *D.C.L. (M.A.)*

Members of the Dunfermline Rugby Club in front of the clubhouse. Many team members had first played the game at their high school. Two such players were Richard Brown and Bill Brabin, who are in this photograph.

ROSYTH BOWLING CLUB, 1956. *D.C.L. (N)*

The Rosyth Bowling Club built a new bowls clubhouse with the financial assistance of the Carnegie Dunfermline Trust. The photograph, taken at the opening of the premises, shows the president of the club, Andrew Blair, with architect Jack Fraser on his right and chairman of the Trust, Ord Cunningham, on his left. When the Carnegie Dunfermline Trust built institutes they included bowling greens. The Rosyth green was built on its present site some distance from the institute.

DUNFERMLINE TENNIS CLUB, 1953–4. *D.C.L.*

The Dunfermline Tennis and Bridge Club has a complex of tennis courts and a clubhouse in Bothwell Street. One well-known person in the photograph is Jimmy Greenwood, Scottish rugby international.

TWO BRIDGES ROAD RACE, 1968. *D.P.G.*
The Two Bridges Road Race, which involves competitors from far and wide, starts and finishes in Dunfermline and is run over a course that includes crossing the Kincardine and Forth Road Bridges.

DUNFERMLINE VIKINGS ICE HOCKEY TEAM, 1950. *D.C.L.*
Many towns in Scotland and England had ice rinks and these were home to ice hockey teams that drew a large number of supporters to every game. Dunfermline had the Vikings and their junior team the Royals. The closure of the ice rink meant no more ice hockey. A large mosaic of a Viking's Head adorned the floor of the entrance vestibule of the Dunfermline ice rink. When the building was demolished this was rescued and was installed on the wall of the ASDA Sports Hall in the Carnegie Centre.

FESTIVALS AND EVENTS

Probably the best-known and best-loved festival in Dunfermline is the annual Schoolchildren's Gala that celebrated its centenary in 2003. The Gala was the inspiration of Mr and Mrs Andrew Carnegie who paid for the first one in August 1903 when the children, who had assembled at the public park, marched through the town to the Urquhart Race Park, a field south of the junction of Coal Road and Lover's Loan, where merry-go-rounds, swing boats, coconut shies, Punch and Judy shows and donkey rides were all provided for their entertainment. The Carnegies stated that 'no expense should be spared'. The following year the Gala was organised and funded by the Carnegie Dunfermline Trust and the venue was Pittencrieff Park, gifted by Mr Carnegie to the people of Dunfermline the previous year.

With the exception of the years during the two world wars when the monies which would have been spent were used to buy ambulances and mobile kitchens, there has been a children's Gala ever since. As the post-war baby boom took effect the number of primary and secondary pupils taking part grew until, in 1947, 8,000 children attended and the Carnegie Dunfermline Trust decided to limit the Gala in 1958 to primary children only. The Gala continued in this form until further changes took place in 1976 when teachers withdrew their support following local government reorganisation and a teachers' strike. A Gala committee assisted by parents took over the task of running the event and Gala day changed to a Saturday. It is still held annually. The Carnegie Dunfermline Trust no longer funds it but provides 'a guarantee against loss'.

The Carnegie Dunfermline Trust organise and fund an annual children's Spring Bulb and Flower Show in Pittencrieff Park when children from the local schools who have purchased bulbs bought from the Trust at discounted prices exhibit the results of their efforts. A competition for nature paintings is held in conjunction with this event that started in 1906.

A Civic Week was held for the first time in 1948 when at the opening Provost Stewart Gellatly stated that its aim was 'to publicise the many attractions of our city and advertise our manufacturers'. The week started with a procession of floats on the first Saturday followed, on Sunday, by a parade of youth organisations to a church

RETAIL TRADERS' EXHIBITION: STEPHEN. *D.C.L. (N)*
In 1953 the Dunfermline Chamber of Commerce promoted an exhibition in the St Margaret's Hall for the retail traders of the town to show their wares and services. Many of these traders are no longer in existence but the firm of Stephen the Bakers is still famous for its pies and steak bridies. One of the posters promoting doughnuts reads 'As you ramble on thru life, brother, whatever be your goal, keep your eye upon the Doughnut and not upon the hole'. If this was the philosophy adopted by Stephen in 1953 it may explain why they are still in business.

service held in Dunfermline Abbey. Various concerts, exhibitions, sporting events and competitions were held during the week and the event finished with the children's Gala. During the early years a reception was held for 'homecomers', former citizens of Dunfermline who had moved from the area but still retained links with Dunfermline and made return visits. Despite changing tastes and frequent loss of interest the Civic Week has survived for more than 50 years and looks set to continue.

While the Carnegie Dunfermline Trust had, from its inception in 1903, actively promoted the arts by sponsoring art exhibitions, orchestral concerts and drama and operatic performances, it was not until 1965 that the Trust considered the possibility of organising a week long Festival of the Arts to include all of these elements. Events were staged at various venues throughout Dunfermline and were well attended. The last Carnegie Festival was held in 1974. The organisation of the festival was taken over by the Dunfermline Association for the Arts and Entertainment but events were only promoted for the next two years. In 1990 the Dunfermline District Arts Council, in association with the District Council, revived it as the Dunfermline District Arts Festival with a format very similar to earlier events but with the inclusion of a Film Festival and incorporating a Jazz Festival which had been started two years previously. Following local government reorganisation, the 1997 event became the Dunfermline and West Fife Arts Festival with events being held at venues throughout the area and the Jazz and Film Festivals were separated from the main event.

The Carnegie Dunfermline Trust have organised and funded a brass band competition for over 30 years and brass bands from far and wide compete for prestigious trophies.

Many royal visits have been made to Dunfermline and Rosyth in the post-war years. The first official visit was in 1948 when King George VI, Queen Elizabeth and Princess Margaret came to Dunfermline. The Duke of Edinburgh inspected the Naval Construction and Research Establishment in 1954. The Queen Mother, as Patron of the National Trust for Scotland, visited Culross the following year and the Queen and Prince Philip embarked on the Royal Yacht *Britannia* at Rosyth for a state visit to Norway, also in 1955. Three years later the City and Royal Burgh received the Queen and Duke of Edinburgh for an official royal visit. They again came to Fife in 1960 for the opening of Kincardine Power Station, in 1961 for the opening of the Lurgi Gas Production Plant at Westfield Ballingry and in 1964 for the opening of the Forth Road Bridge. Prince Charles, Duke of Rothesay, attended the service in Dunfermline Abbey to commemorate the 650th anniversary of the death of King Robert the Bruce and laid a wreath on the tomb beneath the pulpit. The next official royal visit was in 1972 for the 900th anniversary celebration of the founding of Dunfermline Abbey. The Queen opened the Mossmorran Petrochemical Complex at Cowdenbeath during a tour of the plant with the Duke

RETAIL TRADERS'
EXHIBITION: MUIR.
D.C.L. (N)
Muir the music sellers show their range of products: pianos, musical instruments including harmonicas, record players, tape recorders, sheet music and records. Some of the artists shown on the posters such as Gigli and Louis Armstrong are still popular today. In 1953, 45rpm records were introduced as is proclaimed by the poster on the back wall.

of Edinburgh in 1986. The Queen and Prince Philip visited Rosyth to board HMS *Edinburgh* in 1989 when Prince Andrew was a lieutenant on the ship. There were countless other official and unofficial visits when various naval craft were recommissioned and when Prince Charles and Prince Andrew were serving on ships based at the dockyard. Princess Margaret as National Patron for the Margaret 900 celebrations visited Dunfermline in 1993 and in 1996 made a private visit to Abbot House. Her Majesty the Queen and Prince Philip again visited Dunfermline in 2003 for the celebration of the 400th anniversary of the Union of the Crowns in Dunfermline Abbey and, after opening the new children's playground in Pittencrieff Park and meeting representatives from organisations connected with the Carnegie Dunfermline Trust, they attended a lunch in the Music Pavilion to celebrate the centenary of the Trust.

CIVIC WEEK PARADE, 1950. *D.C.L.*
The Civic Week Parade is traditionally the first event of the celebrations. The many floats are provided by trade and industry with others designed and decorated by the various youth and adult organisations in Dunfermline. Dunfermline Co-operative Society was a supporter of the event and they frequently involved their suppliers as has happened here with co-operation between Bibby, supplier of pig meal, and the Co-operative pig farm that supplied the pig and piglets. The slogan 'As sure as 2 and 2 = 4, More Pigs Fed On Bibby's Meal = Quickest Way To Bacon And Pork' is perhaps not the snappiest that could be used.

CIVIC WEEK PARADE, 1953. *M.A. (Ian Terris)*
A tremendous amount of time and effort was put in to producing a decorated float for the Civic Week Parade. Traders had great pride in their entries and perhaps on the day they would be rewarded with the cup for the Best Trade Display. The wedding cake that is being decorated by Ian Terris for this prize-winning entry was built from cardboard cartons that were then covered with icing. To prevent the icing from melting if, as frequently was the case, it rained on the day of the parade, the icing was sprayed with 20 coats of coachbuilder's cellulose. This, unfortunately, then made the icing inedible.

CIVIC WEEK PARADE, 1953. *M.A. (Ian Terris)*
When the cake was completed it was then mounted on the roof of one of the company vans that was itself decorated. Some of the items used were those which firms purchased to decorate their premises for the Queen's Coronation that year.

CIVIC WEEK PARADE, 1955. *D.C.L.*
This is a float advertising Golden Ball Marmalade, a Co-operative product. In 1955 the floats assembled in Dewar Street and proceeded down Chalmers Street, up Bridge Street and up the High Street.

CIVIC WEEK YOUTH PARADE. *D.C.L. (M.A.)*

The leading band for the Civic Week Parade, the youth parade on the first Sunday and the Children's Gala, was the band of HMS *Caledonia*, the Artificer Training School at Rosyth. Here they are leading the youth parade *c.*1952 past the Provost and dignitaries on the Saluting Dais at the Guildhall. In the background is the Royal Hotel that was demolished to allow the building of the first supermarket in Dunfermline by Lipton.

CIVIC WEEK YOUTH PARADE. *D.C.L. (M.A.)*

All of the youth organisations in Dunfermline took part in the Civic Week Youth Parade. The photograph shows the Provost acknowledging the salute by the Colour Party of a Girl Guide Company at the parade *c.*1952.

CIVIC WEEK YOUTH PARADE. *D.C.L.*
A company of girl guides passing the Royal Hotel as they bring up the rear of the parade in 1948.

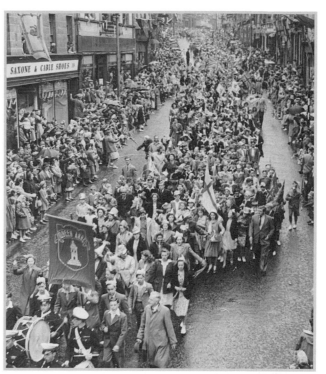

SCHOOL CHILDREN'S GALA DAY. *D.C.L. (Atkinson, S.T.B.)*
Children of Queen Anne's School in the Gala Day Parade of 1948 or 1949. Gala Day was the last Friday of Civic Week and, until 1958 included children from secondary school. Although it would appear to be raining it must not have been sufficient for the event to be called off. Almost the entire population of Dunfermline watched the procession with shops and offices closing while it passed from the public park to Pittencrieff Park.

SCHOOL CHILDREN'S GALA DAY. *D.C.L.*
High School pupils with their teacher, Alex McLennan, in Holyrood Place on Gala Day 1953.

CELEBRATIONS FOR THE WEDDING OF PRINCESS ELIZABETH AND PRINCE PHILIP. *D.C.L. (E.M.C.)*
The children of Talbot Road and probably Lowry Place, taking part in a mock ceremony in the Masonic Hall, Admiralty Road, Rosyth
to mark the royal wedding in November 1947.

STREET PARTY, ROSYTH. *D.C.L. (M.A.)*
Children of Findlay Street, Rosyth, enjoying a street party on the
occasion of the Queen's Coronation in June 1953.

CO-OPERATIVE WEDDING FAYRE. *D.C.L.*
Dunfermline Co-operative staged many events in the Unitas and Randolph Street halls in an attempt to increase business. The photograph shows the main participants in a wedding fayre held in the Unitas Hall in 1960.

CO-OPERATIVE FOOD FAYRE. *D.C.L.*
Miss Peaches and Cream being presented with her sash at her election during the Co-operative Food Fayre in the Unitas Hall in 1965.

OPENING OF THE FORTH ROAD BRIDGE. *McEwan*
After declaring the new Forth Road Bridge open on 4 September 1964, Her Majesty the Queen drove over the bridge to Fife where she unveiled a memorial plaque before returning to South Queensferry aboard one of the ferry boats that would then be redundant.

CITIZEN OF THE YEAR AWARD. *D.C.L. (Norval)*
Dunfermline swimmer Christine Harris was selected for the 1960 Great Britain Olympic swimming team and was chosen as the Dunfermline Citizen of the Year in 1961. Provost Jean Mackie presented her with the trophy on Gala Day in Pittencrieff Park. Also in the presentation party are Andrew Buchanan, Carnegie Trustee, ex-Provosts Allan and Frederick and Rev Andrew Stewart, Minister of Gillespie Memorial Church.

MARGARET 900 CELEBRATIONS. *McEwan.*
1993 was the 900th anniversary of the death of Queen Margaret, later canonized to become Saint Margaret, wife of Malcolm Canmore. Many events were held throughout the year to celebrate this. One such event was a procession through the streets of Dunfermline with participants dressed in period costumes. Here Malcolm Welch takes the part of King Malcolm.

WEST FIFE AGRICULTURAL SHOW. *D.C.L. (M.A.)*
Always a good day out for the farming community in West Fife was the annual Agricultural Show. Various locations were used and in 1958 it was held at Broomhead Park.

ENTERTAINMENT

Television came to Dunfermline in time for the funeral of George VI and the subsequent Coronation of Queen Elizabeth in 1953. Prior to that an ice rink, cinemas, dance halls and theatres were the source of entertainment for the population of Dunfermline and the surrounding area.

The Dunfermline ice rink in Halbeath Road opened just after the outbreak of war in 1939 and provided facilities for ice skating, ice hockey and curling. On frequent occasions a dance floor and bandstand were installed at one end of the rink and apart from the resident band that played for modern and old time dancing, many famous broadcasting bands also visited this venue. A number of Ice Carnivals were staged to full houses and the ice was lifted to allow exhibition tennis to be played. The building also hosted a number of boxing tournaments. Immediately after the war, Canadian ice hockey players came to Scotland to form the basis of the many teams who played in the ice rinks throughout the country. Dunfermline had the Vikings together with the junior team named the Royals and both teams enjoyed national success with fervent support from their fans. Sadly the ice rink did not generate sufficient income to pay for the extensive overhaul required by the freezing plant after its years of use, and it closed in 1955. The building became the stores and headquarters of the South of Scotland Electricity Board. When that body became Scottish Power the facility was transferred to Glenrothes and the ice rink was demolished in 1988 to allow the site to be developed for housing.

When theatre is mentioned in Dunfermline normally thoughts turn to the Carnegie Hall which, since its opening in 1937, has been used for professional and amateur performances of all kinds. However, there were a number of other venues that were also used for these purposes. St Margaret's Hall, adjacent to the Carnegie Library, was used for all types of occasions such as film shows, retail trade shows, orchestral concerts, weekly dancing and boxing tournaments. Indeed it was after one such tournament in 1961 that the hall, which had been purchased by the Dunfermline Town Council in 1948, burned down. Pilmuir Hall, which stood on the corner of Pilmuir Street and Carnegie Street, started life as the first public swimming pool that was gifted to Dunfermline by Andrew Carnegie. It was converted into a public hall after the new baths were built further up Pilmuir Street. The hall was the home of the Scout Gang Show performed annually by the 2nd Fife YMCA troop and in the late 1940s Sunday night shows were staged by performers directed by Dr Sarafin, who taught accordionists in rooms in Carnegie Street. His accordion band and soloists performed in village halls throughout the district. Pilmuir Hall was sold by the Town Council and was converted into offices for the Ministry of Pensions, the purpose for which it was used until its demolition for the improvement of the road junction.

The Dunfermline Co-operative Society owned three halls in town together with one at Townhill and one in Rosyth. The Old Unitas Hall was used for performances given by the amateur dramatic group the Randolph Players. Together with the New Unitas Hall and the Randolph suite of rooms adjoining the Co-operative restaurant, it was used for weddings, funerals and many other types of function. The New Unitas Hall was used for public dances every week. With the demise of the Society in 1990, the buildings were sold and prepared for demolition. The old Unitas Hall was destroyed by fire in 1991.

The former Women's Institute in Pilmuir Street was converted into a youth centre by the Carnegie Dunfermline Trust in 1947 and the Skibo Theatre was fitted out in 1953 and was used as a youth theatre and dance hall by the members for the next 10 years until the building was sold by the Trust. The main commercial theatre in Dunfermline was the Opera House in Reform Street. It opened in 1903 and remained in almost continuous use until it closed in 1955. It housed performances by the great, the not so great and the downright awful, professional and amateur, for over 50 years, but could not meet the competition of television. James Bell and Sons, cabinetmakers, used the building as a workshop and warehouse until 1982 when it was demolished to make way for the new Kingsgate shopping centre. The decorative plasterwork was recovered and was sold to the Asolo Centre for the Performing Arts in Sarasota, Florida, to be incorporated in a new theatre. Dunfermline Opera House lives on. The sale of the plasterwork helped to fund the building of the Tiffany Lounge as part of the Carnegie Hall Complex. As has been referred to earlier, the Carnegie Hall, built by the Carnegie Dunfermline Trust, opened two years before the outbreak of war. It is adjacent to the Music

Institute, Benachie, which had been purchased by the Trust in 1933 to house a Music School that they had started shortly after the Trust had been formed and which had proved to be so popular that it quickly outgrew its existing premises. Thousands of Dunfermline children have been taught music and the playing of musical instruments in Benachie and many have gone on to have a successful musical career. Carnegie Hall, like its counterpart in New York, has hosted every conceivable type of performance and is frequently used as a cinema. It is one of the venues for the Fife Festival of Music when musicians, choirs and soloists compete for various awards. The Dunfermline Brass Band Competition, sponsored by the Carnegie Dunfermline Trust, is held there annually.

The main dance hall in Dunfermline was the Kinema Ballroom that had its entrance in Pilmuir Street. Opened just before the war started, it was the mecca for service personnel during the war and it continued to be the place to go to meet someone of the opposite sex after the war. The competition for the attention of girls sometimes led to confrontation between locals and artificers, known as 'Tiffies', from HMS *Caledonia*, the Naval Training Establishment at Rosyth. The dancehall has been extended several times

and the main entrance is now in Carnegie Drive. The other most notable dancehall was the Co-operative hall in Rosyth, nicknamed the Snake Pit. This too was a favourite of the sailors from Rosyth naval base as well as locals. The Palais at Cowdenbeath and also the one at Aberdour were famous or infamous, depending on one's point of view.

In the post-war and pre-television era there were four cinemas in Dunfermline, the Regal, Alhambra, Cinema and Palace Kinema. There was also the Palace Cinema at Rosyth. Caledonian Associated Cinemas owned the Regal cinema in the High Street and after it closed in 1976 it was destroyed by fire while awaiting demolition in preparation for the Littlewood's development. The Regal was not just a cinema, it also had a very popular restaurant and function suite that was used for weddings and private dances. The Alhambra in Canmore Street, which had originally been built as a theatre/cinema was also owned by CAC and when it ceased being a cinema in 1965 it became a bingo hall. The cinema in East Port had a number of different owners, one of which was CAC who converted it to a three-screen complex in 1982 and renamed it the Orient Express. A further change of ownership saw it once more renamed when it became

ALHAMBRA THEATRE.
D.P.G.
The Alhambra was originally built as a theatre and cinema and is shown in the photograph in 1961 when it was used as a theatre for the three-night presentation of the 'Senior Service Show'. It had nothing to do with the Royal Navy. The show, starring Archie McCulloch and Kathie Kay, was to promote the sale of Senior Service cigarettes. Entry was free and free cigarettes were given to adult members of the audience. The double bill of films showing in the cinema that week were *Two Wives At One Wedding* starring Gordon Jackson and *The Ladies' Man* with Jerry Lewis.

ALHAMBRA BINGO HALL. *D.C.L.*
When the Alhambra ceased to be used as a cinema it was converted into a bingo hall by its owners CAC Ltd. On the 1996 photograph it is named the Caley but the name has changed on a number of occasions over the ensuing years.

REGAL CINEMA. *D.C.L.*
Possibly the saddest loss to the entertainment business in Dunfermline was the closure of the Regal Cinema. The spacious, well-appointed building in the Art Deco Style had a large indoor waiting area for patrons and on the first floor was a restaurant and function hall that was suitable for weddings and dances. It even had its own small car park. The alleyway to the left of the entrance was known as the Regal Close. It led to the car park and Canmore Street and was where McPherson's bookshop was located. The Regal was owned by Caledonian Associated Cinemas who also owned the Cinema and Alhambra, for which an advertisement can be seen inside the entrance.

one of the Robins Group cinemas. It finally closed in 2000 when the new multi-screen Odeon complex opened at the new Halbeath Leisure Park. The Palace Kinema in Pilmuir Street was privately owned and frequently screened less popular films and it was the venue for the Dunfermline and West Fife Film Society showing classic films from 1937–60, excluding the war years. It, like the Cinema and the Palace in Rosyth, was where films were shown for the second run in Dunfermline. It combined being a cinema with being a bingo hall in 1961 and ceased showing films in 1967. It became solely a bingo hall and was finally demolished in 1987. The Palace Cinema in Rosyth was a favourite of sailors from all over the world during the war and continued serving the residents of Rosyth and its visiting naval personnel until 1971. In 1979 it was converted into a public house and club.

Public houses could no doubt be looked on as places of entertainment, but as such their décor and use has changed dramatically from the 'sawdust on the floor, long bar and few seats' to the well furnished places with a pleasant ambience, where women are as welcome as men. Everything including food and entertainment is provided to encourage patrons to continue drinking for as long as the licence allows. Many city centre public houses were demolished to make way for road widening or redevelopment. The Station, Railway, Crown, Northern, Brig and Park taverns, the Unicorn and the Union inns all disappeared in the name of progress. Many others survived but have been frequently modernised with just as frequent changes in their names and would no longer be recognised by their immediate post-war regulars.

The café/ice cream parlours of Maloco, D'Inverno and Alari could also have been considered as places, perhaps not of entertainment, but certainly where people met socially for a chat and exchange of news and where they spent longer than the few minutes which are snatched from a busy shopping routine

THE CINEMA. *D.C.L.*
The last picture house in Dunfermline to close was the Cinema. It struggled to survive until the final nail in the coffin was the opening of the Odeon multi-screen complex at Halbeath. In the 1940s and '50s when the photograph was taken, the attraction of the Cinema was that it was frequently used for the second showing of a film. Therefore, if one missed the first showing in the Regal or Alhambra it would probably return to the Cinema in a few months. The admission prices of 1s 3d for the stalls and 1s 9d for the gallery are painted on either side of the entrance and these are where the queues would form. Performances at all of the picture houses were continuous and patrons could enter at any time during the performance. Unless you were caught by an usherette you could sit twice through a performance consisting of news, cartoon, trailers, feature film and support film.

nowadays. The Abbot's Kitchen in Abbot House is possibly one of the few places in Dunfermline where customers are more leisurely in consuming their meals and snacks and make time to read a newspaper and meet with friends.

Despite the lure of television, there are still a large number of clubs and other organisations offering a diverse range of activities for the residents of Dunfermline and details of meeting days and contacts can be obtained from the Carnegie Library or from the Fife Council website.

The immediate post-war years saw the revival of Boy Scout troops that had been disbanded for the duration of the war. Most churches had Cubs and Scouts, or Lifeboys and Boys' Brigade together with Brownies and Girl Guides. The YMCA and British Legion also had Cub and Scout troops. The coming of television and computers together with a complete change in lifestyle for children of all ages and an

unwillingness of adults to take on the responsibility of running these groups saw the slow death of many of them. Church youth clubs also suffered in the same way. Sport is also a form of entertainment but that is dealt with in separate chapter.

Perhaps not an obvious source of entertainment could be the local newspapers. The *Dunfermline and West Fife Journal*, in its final years printed by R.K. Lindsay, was published from 1851 until 1951. The *Dunfermline Press and West of Fife Advertiser*, in 2003 voted 'Scottish Local Newspaper of the Year' and Fife's best selling weekly, is still going strong and has fulfilled the needs of the local residents for over 140 years. The Dunfermline Press Group also produces a sister publication, the *Fife and Kinross Extra* which is a free issue newspaper.

Another free issue newspaper delivered in the area is the *Herald and Post*, published in Edinburgh by Scotsman publications.

FILM PROMOTIONAL CAMPAIGN. *D.C.L.*
These young cinemagoers are trying out the camp bed that is part of a promotional display for *Carry On Camping* in the foyer of the Regal Cinema *c.*1960.

THE PALACE KINEMA. *D.C.L. (M.A.)*
Manager George Gilchrist never missed a trick with his promotional events. He and a 'spaceman' are trying to entice customers to come to a 1951 performance in the Kinema, as it was locally known. The worst feature of this cinema was that the front row of seats in the stalls was only the width of a walkway from the screen and to sit in this row and see a film was like looking up the face of a cliff. Most of the first few minutes were spent looking back to see when a more favourable seat became vacant. The Kinema was from 1937 to 1960 home to the Dunfermline Film Society that promoted the viewing of foreign and specialist films throughout a winter season. They also promoted the showing of Scottish films during Civic Week.

THE DUNFERMLINE OPERA HOUSE. *D.C.L.*

The Opera House opened in 1903 and closed in 1955 mainly as a result of the competition from television. James Bell and Sons used the building as workshops and showroom for their cabinetmaking business until it was finally demolished in 1982 to allow the Kingsgate shopping project to proceed. For further information on the building and the entertainers who performed there read *100 Years Of The Dunfermline Opera House* by Lilian King, based on research by Brian Nobile.

PILMUIR HALL. *D.P.G.*

Erected as Dunfermline's first swimming baths, which were gifted by Andrew Carnegie, the building became a public hall after the better and more extensive facilities in the new Carnegie Baths opened at the beginning of the 20th century. The hall was used by the 2nd Fife Boy Scouts for their annual 'Gang Show', by Dr Sarafin for his Sunday night pantomimes and variety shows and as an exhibition hall. The building was used by the DHSS as offices for a number of years before being demolished as part of a road improvement scheme in 1963.

ST MARGARET'S HALL. *D.P.G.*

St Margaret's Hall was Dunfermline's primary multi-purpose venue until it was destroyed by fire in 1961 after an evening of boxing. It was used for dances, exhibitions, film shows and concerts and had a large number of rooms that could be rented for meetings. An extension to the Dunfermline Carnegie Library was built on the cleared site.

THE KINEMA BALLROOM. *D.C.L. (E.M.C.)*

Until the new extension that fronts on to Carnegie Drive was built, the entrance to the 'Ballroom' was the one photographed in 1955 in Pilmuir Street showing the entrance price of 2s (10p). This was the only purpose-built dancehall in Dunfermline and it was very popular with naval personnel based at Rosyth.

MR KINEMA BALLROOM. *D.P.G.*
Cecil Hunter, photographed at the opening of an extension to the premises in 1964, managed the Kinema Ballroom for many years.

KINEMA BALLROOM HOSTESSES. *D.C.L. (E.M.C.)*
Two hostesses were employed by the ballroom manager to ensure that everyone enjoyed themselves by bringing couples together for dancing, partnering people who were alone and occasionally defusing potential arguments between rivals. The photograph, taken *c.*1950, shows Lena and Cherry, with the cherry brooch that she always wore.

REGAL CINEMA RESTAURANT. *D.C.L. (John Allan)*
This was a very popular venue in Dunfermline with its dining rooms and function hall that was used for weddings, parties and dances. It was located on the first floor above the entrance foyer of the Regal cinema. The photograph was taken *c.*1950.

RANDOLPH STREET HALL. *D.C.L.*
The Dunfermline Co-operative Society had a number of halls in its Randolph Street complex. Until the Unitas Hall was opened, the main function hall was the Randolph Street Hall that was used for all types of events. When it opened in 1888 it was stated that its design was such that it was 'thoroughly fireproof' but this was disproved when the by then disused offices and hall were severely damaged by a fire in 1991. The photograph shows the hall after it had been modernised in 1959.

JIM BROWN'S DANCE BAND. *D.C.L. (M.A.)*
There were many popular semi-professional dance bands playing in the various venues in Dunfermline and the surrounding area. One such band was the Jim Brown Dance Band, photographed in 1955.

DAVID GRAY AND HIS DANCE BAND. *D.C.L. (M.A.)*
Hairdresser David Gray led another of the popular dance bands, photographed at a performance *c.*1950.

NAZARETH. *D.C.L.*
None of the bands and entertainers in Dunfermline in the 1950s could have imagined what it would be like to make it 'big time' like the local group Nazareth shown on a 1996 publicity photograph.

ROSYTH PIPE BAND. *D.C.L. (M.A.)*
Dunfermline and Rosyth each had pipe bands that took part in the various competitions and events throughout Scotland. Taken in 1977, the photograph shows the Rosyth Pipe Band in full regalia in front of the Rosyth Institute.

EAST END PARK. *D.C.L.*
In 1962 work started on the building of a new stand. The stand was built on the south side of the ground on the site of the old corrugated iron stand and the photograph shows the commencement of the erection of the steel framework over the wooden huts that had for many years served as changing rooms and offices.

THE JUBILEE. *D.C.L. (Arthur Davis)*
St Margaret Villa was purchased by the Dunfermline Football Supporters' Club and was renamed the Jubilee Club. It was extremely successful for many years and was extended twice to provide two function halls and bars for the membership. This membership dwindled towards the end of the 1990s and rising debts forced the closure, sale and subsequent demolition of the premises. Retirement flats were built on the site.

THE CROWN TAVERN. *D.C.L.*
Dunfermline lost a number of public houses as a result of town centre development and road junction improvements. The Crown Tavern was located on the corner of Pittencrieff Street and Chalmers Street and was demolished in 1971. Despite this work being carried out the photograph shows that the adjacent shops were still trading. The area is now the site of Canon Lynch Court.

AULD TOLL TAVERN. *D.C.L.*
While all around it has changed, the Auld Toll Tavern still operates into its second century. It was originally known as Jennie Rennie's Pub and the lane on the left was Jennie Rennie's Lane leading to the Grange Road. The name was used for one of the new roads in the Izatt Avenue housing scheme.

COOKERY CLASS. *D.C.L.*
In 1952 cooking with modern gas appliances is being demonstrated in the lecture theatre on the first floor of the Gas Company, later the Gas Board showrooms in Canmore Street. This was to stimulate sales of sophisticated new gas cookers.

DUNFERMLINE CINE CLUB. *Peter Leslie.*

A cine club was formed in Dunfermline *c*.1952 and met in the youth centre in Pilmuir Street. The membership soon outgrew the premises and the club moved to Abbot House. Many competitions were organised throughout the season and the photograph, taken *c*.1971, shows winners with their trophies at the annual prize-giving ceremony. The advent of the video camera saw a decline in the use of film and the club was revived as the Camcorder Club.

ROSYTH SCOUTS. *D.C.L.*

The members of the 61st Fife St John's RC Rosyth Scout Troup proudly show the trophies won in 1957.

DUNFERMLINE SCOUTS. *D.C.L.*
Members of the 2nd Fife YMCA Scout Troup at their annual camp at Crook of Devon *c.*1945. Many of those present are named on the back of the original photograph.

GILLESPIE MEMORIAL CHURCH GUIDE COMPANY. *D.C.L. (M.A.)*
At the time of this photograph in 1952, most Dunfermline churches had Girl Guide Companies and Brownie Packs for the youth of the church.

GILLESPIE MEMORIAL CHURCH BOYS' BRIGADE COMPANY. *D.C.L. (M.A.)*
The equivalent organisations within churches for boys were Scouts and Cubs or, as in the case of the Gillespie Memorial Church in 1952, Boys' Brigade and Lifeboys.

TIFFANY LOUNGE. *D.C.L. (E.M.C.)*
It had long been the aim of 'The Friends of Carnegie Hall' to have a bar and café built adjacent to Carnegie Hall as an added facility for theatregoers. In 1993 the Tiffany lounge was opened. It had been built with funds raised from sponsors and grants after a base funding was provided by the sale of the plasterwork from the Dunfermline Opera House to the Assolo Centre for Performing Arts in Sarasota, Florida. A stained-glass window gifted by Andrew Carnegie in memory of his family was relocated from the Carnegie Hall into the lounge thus giving it its name. The lounge is open for snacks and meals on weekdays and Saturdays.

**ROTARY CLUB OF
DUNFERMLINE**

*Charity
Ball*

Programme

1 Quickstep
2 Modern Waltz
3 Slow Foxtrot
4 Canadian Barn Dance
5 The Twist
6 Hesitation Waltz
7 Quickstep
8 Paul Jones (Modern)
9 Country Dance
10 Slow Foxtrot
11 Quickstep
12 Eightsome Reel
13 Medley
14 Circle Waltz
15 Twist and Shake
16 Dashing White Sergeant
17 Quickstep
18 Spanish Circle Waltz

Programme

19 Quickstep
20 Paul Jones (Old Medley)
21 Slow Foxtrot
22 Strip the Willow
23 Cha-Cha
24 Quickstep (Statue) Prize
25 Valeta Waltz
26 Twist
27 Eightsome Reel
28 Paul Jones (Modern)
29 Modern Waltz
30 Foxtrot (Spot)
31 Samba
32 Slow Foxtrot
33 Twist
34 Pride of Erin
35 Quickstep
36 Last Waltz

GOD SAVE THE QUEEN

ROTARY CHARITY BALL. *McEwan.*
The three months from November were the season for dances and balls. These formal affairs were generally held in the Unitas Hall or, as in the case of the Rotary Ball, the Music Pavilion of Pittencrieff Park. The venue for the Hospitals' Ball in 1966 was the Kinema Ballroom. This late 1960s programme shows that the Twist had arrived, even at formal dances.

TOURISM AND HERITAGE

There has been a constant endeavour since 1945 to increase the profile of the City and Royal Burgh of Dunfermline as a historical tourist attraction with a varied degree of success.

In 1965 the Carnegie Dunfermline Trust embarked on a scheme to erect 'blue plaques' on several of the important sites throughout the town. The first sites chosen were Crosswynd, East Port, Abbey Wall and Nether Yett. The Carnegie Birthplace and Museum was given a makeover in 1984 to make it more user friendly. This was a forerunner of the events to be held in 1985. As part of the celebration of the 150th anniversary that year of the birth of Andrew Carnegie, the Carnegie Dunfermline Trust commissioned Michael Quinion Associates to devise a scheme to promote tourism based on the heritage of Dunferm-line. Among the suggestions that they put forward was the proposal to erect orientation boards at car parks, the bus station and the railway station. Twenty-five places of historic interest would be denoted by marker plaques, a heritage booklet would be on sale at the tourist office and local shops and a teacher's resource pack would be available for all local schools. Over the years most of the plaques have disappeared and the orientation panels became obsolete. These panels were replaced with up-to-date maps and information panels in 2000. In 2004 Fife Council, in collaboration with the Carnegie Dunfermline Trust and with additional grant funding available, are planning to erect new plaques at the historic sites. However, one innovation from 1985 has endured. The Carnegie Dunfermline Trust embarked on a scheme for training a corps of Heritage

INAUGURATION OF THE DUNFERMLINE HERITAGE SCHEME, 1985. *D.P.G.*

In 1985 the Carnegie Dunfermline Trust as part of their celebrations for the 150th Anniversary of the birth of Andrew Carnegie, promoted a scheme to raise the profile of Dunfermline as a tourist destination. They employed a firm of consultants whose proposal for plaques on the important buildings together with an explanatory booklet was accepted. They also suggested that a team of Heritage Guides should be recruited and trained. Guides would conduct tourists on free walks around the historic sites in Dunfermline. Inauguration of the scheme was carried out by Dick Douglas MP, Provost Bob Mill, George Adamson, Trust chairman and fellow trustees in July 1985. Walks take place each Sunday from April to October and by special arrangement. One of the guides, Jack Pryde, suggested to the Trust that a walk should be undertaken on the most appropriate day after New Year's Day and this has been a successful addition to the programme with up to 400 people taking part one year. The New Year walk finishes at the Carnegie Birthplace where welcome refreshments are provided.

DUNFERMLINE MERCAT CROSS. *McEwan.*
Traditionally the centre of the market area in a town, Dunfermline's 17th-century Mercat Cross is here shown in its original position. The Cross was on a site beside the Guildhall and was temporarily moved to Maygate to allow the paving work to be carried out prior to pedestrianisation of the High Street. Before being returned to its final resting place, a new sandstone shaft was fitted and the original shaft has been erected in the garden of Abbot House.

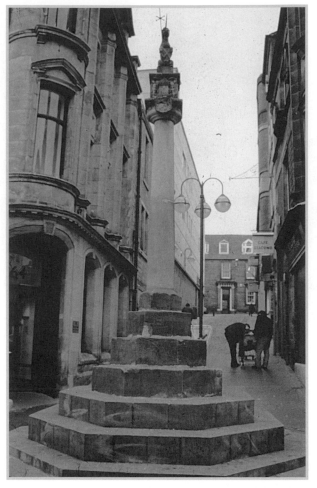

Guides to take visitors on free guided walks through Dunfermline throughout the summer and on other occasions by special arrangement. Further guides have been added to the corps each year after suitable training and examination before receiving their badge and umbrella. One walk which has become an institution is the one held on the most suitable day after New Year when up to 400 people have been known to turn up at the Mercat Cross for a leisurely stroll to see in the New Year.

The Dunfermline Tourist Association was formed in 1961. After occupying a small office at the entrance to the Chalmers Street car park and then a room in Abbot House, the Tourist Information Centre was opened in Maygate in 1993. The organisation was later taken over by the Fife Tourist Board and moved to new premises at No.1 High Street in 2001.

Historic Scotland and its predecessors have continuously carried out improvements to the properties under its care in order that visitors may more easily understand the history of the Abbey, Palace and Monastery. In 1989, with the aid of a grant from the Carnegie Dunfermline Trust, public access to the undercroft of the Monastery and to the royal apartments in the Palace was improved. Interpretation panels were also installed at strategic points throughout the properties. The Abbey Nave was provided with improved lighting in 2002. A custodian is on duty and there is a shop selling a limited range of souvenirs.

The Abbey Church is open from April to October and provides guides for tourists; it too has a shop selling souvenirs. The pedestrianisation of Dunfermline High Street saw the installation of poles to which banners depicting historical events could be attached.

Following a public meeting in February 1989, the Dunfermline Heritage Trust was incorporated in 1990. Its objects were 'to advance the education of the public generally and particularly the inhabitants of Dunfermline and district by the preservation,

THE CANNON. *McEwan.*
The original site for the cannon, a gift from the Carron Ironworks in the 18th century, was in the corner of the pavement at the City Chambers designed to prevent vehicles from cutting the corner. During the war it was a hazard to pedestrians in the blackout and was moved into the corner of the building. It was removed when new paving was being laid but after pressure was put on the local authority it was returned to a place of honour in Bridge Street.

ABBOT HOUSE HERITAGE CENTRE. *McEwan.*

The Carnegie Dunfermline Trust that already owned the east wing of the building purchased the two dwelling houses that formed the bulk of Abbot House in 1948. After proposals to return the house to its original state were abandoned the building was eventually converted in 1961–3 into meeting rooms that could be rented by clubs and individuals. It was also the meeting place and library of the Dunfermline Presbytery. Its use declined in the 1980s and, following the formation of the Dunfermline Heritage Trust in 1989, plans were drawn up for its conversion into a Heritage Centre. The Carnegie Dunfermline Trust gifted the building to the Heritage Trust and it opened as the Abbot House Heritage Centre at Easter 1995. It has since won many awards for its imaginative presentation of the history of Dunfermline. During the conversion work evidence was discovered which allowed part of the structure to be dated as 15th century.

restoration, enhancement, display and maintenance of features and objects of historical, social, industrial, educational, artistic and ecological interest in or germane to the Dunfermline area, and to promote a wider appreciation of the history, social development and heritage of the area'. In furtherance of these aims the Heritage Trust would provide and maintain a Heritage Centre or centres. The Abbot House Heritage Centre opened on 14 April 1995. The Carnegie Dunfermline Trust gifted the building and funding for the project was obtained from public and private sources. The centre has received many awards for the quality and imagination of the conversion of the 15th-century building into a tourist attraction of which the people of Dunfermline can be proud and which draws visitors from nearly every country in the world.

Following the formation of the Chalmers Street car park, several attempts were made to attract members of the public to St Margaret's Cave, which was now accessed by means of an underground tunnel. The cave finally became a tourist attraction when a new entrance was built and lighting and information boards were installed in the tunnel. The cave was officially opened in 1993 during the Margaret 900 celebrations. A tourist bus service that collects passengers at the railway station and transports them around the main tourist attractions before completing its circular route at the station was inaugurated in 2002. The project was partly financed by a grant of £10,000 from the Carnegie Dunfermline Trust.

Accommodation for visitors to the west Fife area has been improved greatly with the building of new hotels and the conversion of properties into hotels, guesthouses and bed and breakfast establishments.

WAR ROOM MURAL, ABBOT HOUSE HERITAGE CENTRE. *McEwan.*
Many local artists were employed to carry out restoration work and create new works of art for the various rooms in Abbot House. One such artist was Shona McEwan, who restored the mural by Alan Ronald in the War Room.

HRH Princess Margaret visits Abbot House Heritage Centre. *D.P.G.*

In 1996 HRH Princess Margaret paid a private visit to Abbot House where she was guided through the various rooms by Margaret Dean, chairman of the Dunfermline Heritage Trust, and met the volunteers who act as guides, serve in the café and staff the shop every day of the year except Christmas and New Year's Day. She was presented with a posy of flowers by the daughters of Peter Ranson, architect for the conversion of the house into a Heritage Centre.

The Countess of Elgin at the official opening of St Margaret's Cave. *D.C.L.*

When the car park was created in the ravine of the Town Burn the cave where it is thought St Margaret carried out her private devotions was buried and access to the cave was by a tunnel. In order to encourage more visitors the tunnel was refurbished with improved lighting and interpretation panels. A new entrance building was erected and in 1993 during the celebrations to mark the 900th anniversary of the death of Queen Margaret the building was opened by the Countess of Elgin. A time capsule containing details of the celebrations was buried near the entrance building.

TWINNING AND FRIENDSHIP LINKS

The system of twinning of towns, cities and communities was not an institution first initiated by the EEC or European Community as it is now called. Dunfermline can claim to have the oldest twinning in Europe dating from 1945.

Before hostilities had ceased in World War Two, representatives of all youth organisations in Dunfermline met in 1944 and decided to adopt a town that had been under German occupation. An approach was made to the Norwegian authorities and the Scottish representative of the Norwegian Ministry of Information suggested that Trondheim would be a suitable choice because it had many similarities to Dunfermline. Both had been ancient capitals, both had churches dating back to the 12th century and they both had a population of around 55,000. The 'Adoption Ceremony' was held in the Regal cinema on 6 May 1945, two days before the liberation of Norway.

On the first of many exchange visits between the two cities, a party of 22 young people from Trondheim visited Dunfermline in 1946 and were given a civic reception and shown around the tourist spots in the area. The first return visit was made in 1948 when Miss Nettie Dick, Carnegie Youth Centre leader, accompanied 20 members of the Youth Centre to Trondheim. Provost Robertson was allowed to take the Provost's robes and chain of office on a formal visit in 1952 and Provost Frederick and the town clerk also visited in 1958. Mayor Olav Gjaerevoll returned the compliment in 1959 and the naming of a street in the Abbeyview housing estate, Trondheim Parkway, further strengthened the link which continued undiminished until the retirement in 1972 of Miss Dick, who was awarded the King Olaf's Medal by the King of Norway that year for her services to Norway and the link.

With local government reorganisation in which the City and Royal Burgh became Dunfermline District, the leader of the new administration thought the link 'had become tenuous and was often an excuse for a junket at the expense of the ratepayers, something he would guard against'.

During the Margaret 900 Celebrations to mark the

TRONDHEIM VISITORS. *D.C.L. (N)*
A party of young people, photographed with their Dunfermline hosts and the chairman and trustees of the Carnegie Dunfermline Trust, were the first to participate in an exchange visit in 1946 between Dunfermline and Trondheim. A twinning agreement to promote friendship and cultural exchange had been signed between the two cities the previous year. This unique bond has led to exchange visits, in private and official capacities, continuing for nearly 60 years.

anniversary of the death of Queen Margaret, Bishop Mario Conti (now Archbishop of Glasgow) presented a statuette of St Margaret to the Catholic community in Trondheim.

While the link had never really been severed, in 1996 the Trondheim–Dunfermline Twinning Link was set up by a group of interested people with a view to the link being re-established and strengthened. This became the Twinning Association a year later. The Carnegie Dunfermline Trust gave a grant to enable the 'Lifeline' Art Group, set up by art teachers in Dunfermline to present an exhibition in Abbot House in collaboration with art students from Trondheim visiting Dunfermline. A further opportunity to strengthen the link came with the 1,000th birthday of Trondheim in 1997 when Torcail Stewart, a student crew member on the *Malcolm Miller* which was participating in the Tall Ships Race, delivered greetings and a copy of the *Ballad of Sir Patrick Spens* from the people of Dunfermline. He received in return a bound volume of the *History of Trondheim* that was deposited in the Carnegie Library.

Fife Council acknowledged the existence of the link by adding Trondheim 997–1997 to the welcome signs at the entrances to Dunfermline.

This link was established and maintained by the determination of the youth, citizens and councillors of the City and Royal Burgh without the assistance of funding from the European Union but the establishment of similar links became less likely when the Union adopted a policy of encouraging twinning between towns and cities in member states. With this

policy came the promise of monies to fund the ventures.

The Dunfermline District Council gratefully accepted this carrot when Provost Les Wood set the official seal on a twinning agreement with Wilhelmshaven in 1979. This agreement brought a cheque for £2,500 from the Wilhelmshaven Savings Bank. The money was to be spent on restoration work and was donated to the St Peter's Church, Inverkeithing, Tower Restoration Fund. Twinning was also thought to hold the key to obtaining funds from the European Social Fund that would be put to schemes to train the young jobless. Wilhelmshaven was already linked to Vichy in France and because of this Dunfermline also claimed a link but this seems to have foundered.

A further twinning occurred in 1991 with Logrono in northern Spain in 1991 and, at the instigation of the council leader who thought such a thing was an excuse for a junket, with Albufiera in Portugal in 1995–6.

The Sister Cities Association of Sarasota, Florida, US made approaches to various authorities in Dunfermline with a view to establishing Dunfermline as a 'Sister City'. Sarasota was founded by Scots and still has a strong association with Scotland. The fact that the plasterwork from the Dunfermline Opera House was installed in one of their theatres made the choice of Dunfermline an obvious one. Several visits have been made to and from Sarasota and the scheme has the backing of Fife Council. A scroll commemorating the agreement was presented to Dunfermline in 2003 and is on show in the Dunfermline Carnegie Library.

SARASOTA, SISTER CITY. *Linda Rosenbluth.*
Sarasota, Florida has a strong Caledonian connection and the plasterwork from the Dunfermline Opera House was installed in the Assolo Centre for the Performing Arts. All of this led to Dunfermline being chosen by Sarasota to become a 'Sister City'. After visits to America by representatives of various organisations in Dunfermline and reciprocal visits by officials of the Sarasota Sister Cities Organisation to Scotland, a formal agreement was signed in 2002 in the Van Wezel Performing Arts Hall in Sarasota.

TRONDHEIM PARKWAY. *D.C.L.*
As a symbol of the friendship between Trondheim and Dunfermline the Town Council decided to name two streets in the Abbeyview housing estate Trondheim Parkway and Trondheim Place. Eight of these five-storey blocks of flats and maisonettes, photographed *c.*1960, were built along the north side of Trondheim Parkway and traditional blocks of flats were built by the Scottish Special Housing association on the south side. All of the houses along the street were demolished to allow a regeneration programme for the area to be commenced but by 2004 no progress had been made with rebuilding.

TRONDHEIM TWINNING. *D.P.G.*
Netty Dick was appointed by the Carnegie Dunfermline trust to be Youth Leader in charge of the new Youth Centre which would open in the former Women's Institute in Pilmuir Street in 1947. As such she was responsible for arranging the exchange visits between the youth of Trondheim and the youth of Dunfermline that helped to maintain the first twinning link to be established in Europe. She was awarded the King Olaf's Medal by the King of Norway in 1970 for the work she had done in promoting and maintaining the link and is shown receiving her medal from the representative of the King. She was presented to the King on her next visit to Norway to receive his personal thanks.

SHOPPING

The central shopping area of Dunfermline remained relatively unchanged, with the exception of ownership and tenancy changes, until the 1960s. Major changes started with the demolition of the Royal Hotel in the High Street to allow the building of Dunfermline's first supermarket, opened by Lipton in 1967.

This started the chain reaction that, in 1970, saw the building of a shop for Mothercare in Bridge Street, the rebuilding of the premises occupied by Boots in the High Street and a major refurbishment of the Woolworth store, also in the High Street. The next large-scale development was the demolition of the Regal cinema and many other properties in the High Street to allow building of a Littlewoods store and a complex of shops in the High Street and New Row in 1976. Out-of-town shopping was heralded by the building of a superstore for Fine Fare in 1975 at St Leonard's Street on part of the site of the St Leonard's linen factory. The Carnegie Retail Park was built on the site of the Dunfermline Upper Station and an ASDA superstore and other retail outlets were built on a retail park at Halbeath.

In order that shopping in town could be made more attractive a large shopping mall was planned. This involved the demolition of many properties between the High Street and Carnegie Drive to allow for the new Kingsgate Shopping Centre to be built. Dunfermline entered the new era for shopping when the centre opened in 1985. The Dunfermline Co-operative Society also embarked on a redevelopment plan at this time and built a new supermarket adjacent to their existing complex in Randolph Street. The project was overtaken by the demise of co-operative societies throughout the country and was finally doomed when the local society sold out to the Co-operative Retail Group who promptly closed all of the shops in the Randolph Street complex. Many schemes have been put forward for the complete redevelopment of the area with the latest proposals being submitted in 2003.

Pedestrianisation of the main shopping streets of Dunfermline in 1993 has, in theory, made it safer and more pleasant for shoppers.

OPERA HOUSE FIRE CURTAIN. *M.A. (Ian Terris)*
Businesses in Dunfermline vied for the prize position of centre advertisement on the fire curtain in Dunfermline Opera House. It was like being 'top of the bill'. This curtain was lowered during the interval at every performance, so the patrons could not fail to read the adverts while passing the time until the interval was over and the entertainment began again. Stephen the Bakers tried for many years before wresting this spot from their rival Allan, who were also bakers.

APPIN CRESCENT. *D.C.L.*

The 1972 photograph shows the Park Tavern and John Donald (Draper) Ltd which together with a grocer's shop all fell victim to the bulldozer to allow the creation of the Sinclair Gardens Roundabout. John Donald, by then run by Ian Donald whose car had the appropriate registration number SEM 1T, the old Scots word for a vest, relocated to the recently vacated shop of Coull and Matthew in Chalmers Street.

BONNAR STREET. *D.C.L.*

The buildings on the left of the photograph taken *c.*1970 are still unchanged, except for tenants, but those on the west side of Bonnar Street and New Row have all gone. In those days it was safe to leave a pram, probably with a baby in it, outside a shop and there was a policeman on points duty to see to the safety of motorists and pedestrians. It was also possible to park in the street, but it could be that the notice displayed on the lamppost on the right was intimation that parking restrictions were about to be introduced.

INGLIS STREET. *D.C.L.*
This part of Inglis Street disappeared and the small shops and businesses moved to alternative premises shortly after this photograph was taken in 1981. They, and the Dunfermline Opera House seen in the background, were demolished for the building of the Kingsgate Shopping Mall.

QUEEN ANNE STREET. *D.C.L.*
Another street, photographed *c.*1981, which disappeared in the redevelopment, was Queen Anne Street. The Union Inn was run on the 'Gothenburg' principle where profits were used for the good of the local community. R.C. Ferguson, florists, moved firstly to Pilmuir Street and then to East Port. The vast garage premises of Goodall started life as stables and were vacated when the business merged with the Fife Motor Company in Halbeath Road.

QUEEN ANNE STREET. *F.M.S.*

The same area two years later when demolition had started. The Union Inn had already been demolished and a start has been made on the Ferguson shop.

REFORM STREET. *D.C.L.*

Some of the countless small shops in Dunfermline that provided a living for their owners and staff can be seen on the photograph of the junction of Reform Street and Pilmuir Street in the 1960s. This one short street had public houses on three of its corners, the Opera House, a school, for which the warning sign can be seen, McBay's fish shop at one end and Ramage's bakers shop at the other end of the north side together with a number of small shops selling a variety of goods and services. On the south side Dobbie's saddlery and leather shop was where many school children obtained their first school satchel.

HOSPITAL HILL. *D.C.L.*

The Burmah garage and filling station and Margot's hairdressing salon occupied these premises on the corner of Tollgate and Hospital Hill in 1971. The price of petrol was fairly uniform then but garages lured customers with special offers such as the one shown on the poster 'One unique egg cup with every 4 gallons'.

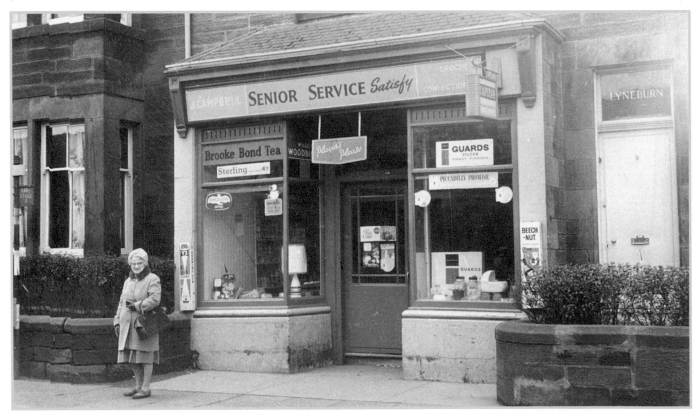

ST LEONARD'S STREET. *D.C.L.*

In 1973, three years after this photograph was taken, the Fine Fare Supermarket was built on the site of the St Leonard's Infant School and it is doubtful if this shop and others like it in the street would have survived. They and the surrounding houses that they had served were demolished for the formation of a dual carriageway.

HOSPITAL HILL. *D.C.L.*
Laidlaw's Garage, formerly Normand's who also had a showroom opposite the Dunfermline High School, is photographed in 1971 being demolished after the firm had moved into new premises in Halbeath Road. A filling station was built on the site but that closed in 2001.

PITTENCRIEFF STREET. *D.C.L. (M.A.)*
In 1952 bookmakers were turf accountants or, as Eddie Kane describes himself on the window of his imposingly named 'Highlander House' premises in Pittencrieff Street, commission agents. Steedman's barber's shop was next door and clients could peruse the newspapers provided there, have a haircut and shave before nipping into the bookies to place their bet or hand in their football coupon. They then had the choice of walking up Pittencrieff Street to the Crown Tavern or down the street to the Glen Tavern for their favourite tipple while waiting for the result of the race when, if they had been lucky, they could collect their winnings.

REGAL CLOSE. *D.C.L. (E.M.C.)*

McPherson's shop selling new and second hand books together with stationery of all kinds was located in the Regal Close until the Cinema and the immediate area was acquired for development by Littlewoods. The business moved to Chalmers Street where it remained until the retirement of the owners Mr and Mrs Forrester.

MALOCO'S ICE CREAM PARLOUR. *D.C.L.*

In the 1950s as international travel became more common, people became used to frequenting cafés where coffee or tea could be drunk in a comfortable atmosphere which was less formal than the tea rooms of the Co-operative or Bruce. Maloco's Ice Cream Parlour was extended to provide such a facility. A billiards and snooker hall was accessed via the alley to the right of the café. This closed after being substantially damaged in the fire which destroyed the derelict Regal cinema and St Paul's Church. The shop front and ground floor café area were modernised before this photograph was taken *c.*1970.

Icᴇ Cʀᴇᴀᴍ Vᴇɴᴅᴏʀ. *D.C.L. (E.M.C.)*
Maloco's ice cream cart is photographed, possibly on Gala day, in 1951 on its allotted site on the roadway leading to the Carnegie statue. Each of the ice cream shops in Dunfermline would have a booth allocated to them in Pittencrieff Park on that day.

Pʜᴏᴛᴏᴄʀᴀꜰᴛ. *D.C.L. (M.A.)*
The studio and shop premises in Chalmers Street of Morris Allan are here photographed in 1965. Morris was a freelance professional photographer who carried out commissions all over the country for clients. He gained fame and notoriety for his various 'scoops' the most famous of which were his photographs of the Russian satellites, Sputniks I, II and III over Dunfermline. A move into filming for television meant frequent attendances at Dunfermline Athletic football matches. When the Fife Schools Television Service opened in premises at Queen Anne School and later in part of Pittencrieff School, Morris Allan was appointed to take charge of the project which also involved Eric Holmes, Bill Fyfe and Jimmy Priddy. When Morris retired he presented his extensive archive of negatives, glass plate and film based, to the Local History Department of the Dunfermline Carnegie Library. A selection of them is used in this publication.

QUEEN ANNE STREET. *D.C.L.*

The jewellery and antiques shops of Felix Hudson were located in the part of Queen Anne Street that was formerly known as Rotten Row. He was an authority on antique clocks and published books on the subject. The premises above the shops were where R.K. Lindsay printed the *Dunfermline Journal*. They were later used as a fitness centre and gym.

DOUGLAS STREET. *D.C.L. (M.A.)*

Tommy Black was a well-known trader in Dunfermline with his fishmongers and greengrocers in Douglas Street. He also opened a market in the former St Andrew's South Church in St Margaret's Street. Douglas Street was crowded on the day that he held a celebration sale for his silver jubilee in February 1960 selling goods at 1935 prices.

EAST PORT. *D.C.L. (E.M.C.)*

The photograph taken in the early 1950s shows the barrier at the bus stops in East Port where passengers could queue in safety. The numerous small shops in the street at that time did a good trade with the people waiting for a town or country service bus.

NEW ROW. *D.C.L.*

There were a number of shops between Priory Lane and Canmore Street. The Licensed Grocery of Ian Christie was on the corner of Priory Lane. It was previously owned by Dick's Co-operative Society. Douglas Arneil and his wife operated a ladies' and gents' hairdresser in the adjacent shops. The photograph was taken *c.*1960 and the properties were later demolished to allow improvements to the road junction.

BANNERMAN STREET. *D.C.L. (E.M.C.)*
Street traders were still using horses and carts for more than a decade after this photograph was taken. William Best can be seen at his Bannerman Street stables with his entry for a parade either at Civic Week or the local agricultural show. Many of the traders changed to motorised transport in later years but some took the opportunity to retire.

THE FIRST SUPERMARKET.
D.C.L.
Supermarket shopping came to Dunfermline *c.*1966 when Lipton, who had a traditional grocery shop at the west end of the High Street, demolished the Royal Hotel, east of the Guildhall, and a supermarket with loading access from Canmore Street was built on the site.

BUCHANAN'S SHOE SHOP. *D.C.L. (N)*
The best-known traditional shoe shop in Dunfermline High Street was owned by Andrew Buchanan. The shop stocked quality boots and shoes for ladies and gentlemen. The window display shows a variety of Dunlop Wellington boots and a moisture absorbent pack to be inserted in boots and shoes after use named Dri-pac telling customers to 'be dry shod tomorrow'. Buchanan's and the Co-operative Shoe Shop had X-ray machines, supplied by Clarks Shoes, which could be used to check the fit of shoes.

HIGH STREET. *Ian Terris.*
A photograph of the High Street, possibly early on a Sunday morning in the 1950s, showing Baird's Shoe Shop, William Stephen's Baker's Shop, John Webster's Fruit and Flower Shop and the James Bonnar's Ironmonger's Shop.

IRONMONGERS, 1. *D.P.G.*
Dunfermline had a large number of ironmongers who sold all manner of tools and other requirements for the many tradesmen operating in Dunfermline. Perhaps the best known was James Bonnar and Sons in the High Street. As well as a vast range of ironmongery and tools, the shop stocked a large selection of items for the home. More importantly for the children of the town, they were stockists for Meccano, Hornby and Dinky toys. The moving models that formed their Christmas display were an attraction for children and adults. The shop closed when the owner retired.

IRONMONGERS, 2. *D.P.G.*
Coull and Matthew moved into these premises that were a replacement for the shop that was demolished for the construction of the Louise Carnegie Gates of Pittencrieff Park. The business became Burt and Graham and relocated to smaller premises on the other side of the street. It continued there until the retirement of Alec Burt.

IRONMONGERS, 3. *D.P.G.* Souness operated in premises opposite the entrance to the Chalmers Street car park. Many of the manufacturers whose goods are displayed here in 1963 are still supplying ironmongers' shops. One sales method that could not be used today is the displaying of ladders that are simply tied to hooks at the shop doorway.

IRONMONGERS, 4. *D.P.G.* Watt and Dewar is the only one of the ironmongers photographed in 1963 for National Hardware Week which is still trading. They moved from these premises in East Port to the New Row when the building was acquired for the building of branch premises for the Bank of Scotland. The shop, run by Jim Craig and his wife, is an Aladdin's cave with everything from the proverbial needle to an anchor. In 1963 it was possible to safely display a range of cutlery outside the shop.

FIFE MOTOR COMPANY. *D.C.L. (N)*
The garage, showroom and filling station of the Fife Motor Company was located in Halbeath Road immediately west of East End Park. The company was the appointed Morris and Morris Commercial dealer for West Fife. Vans, such as the one on this 1960 photograph, were often bought as a chassis to which a coach built body would be added by one of the coachbuilders in Dunfermline. The Fife Motor Company also had a showroom, garage and filling station in St Margaret's Street south of the St Margaret's Hotel, later the site of Goldberg's shop and now the location of a nightclub. The company merged with Goodall and were subsequently taken over by Taggart.

CANMORE STREET. *McEwan.*
This was the showroom and offices of the Dunfermline Town Council Gas Company and after nationalisation, Scottish Gas. It was opened in May 1939 and had a lecture and demonstration theatre on the first floor. The building was sold when Scottish Gas moved to smaller premises in the High Street in 1975 and became the Faith Mission Book Shop.

FINE FARE SUPERMARKET. *D.C.L. (M.A.)*

The fresh meat display at the Fine Fare supermarket in St Leonard's Street shows how prices have changed in 25 years. 1978 was a time when customers were purchasing meat in bulk to fill their new freezers, sometimes sharing the cost of a half side of beef or half lamb with a relative or neighbour.

HALFORDS, BRIDGE STREET. *D.C.L. (E.M.C.)*

While the photograph is not dated it was possibly taken in the 1970s in the run up to Christmas when manager Jim Latimer and his staff were preparing for the rush to buy car and cycle accessories as Christmas presents. The company moved to a purpose-built store in the Carnegie Drive Retail Park.

HIGH STREET. *D.C.L.*

With the exception of the Co-operative shop with its many departments, shops sold exclusively menswear or ladies' fashions and accessories. Dunfermline had many of these such as Budge, Miss Forrest, Hutton and Miss Aitken, whose shop is photographed *c.*1950.

EAST PORT. *D.C.L. (E.M.C.)*

Showrooms and offices were built for the Fife Electric Power Company in 1938 but were not completed. On the outbreak of war the showroom was converted into an air raid shelter. It was fitted out as a showroom for the South of Scotland Electricity Board after the industry was nationalised in 1948. It remained in use until 1994 when the privatised Scottish Power moved out and the building was sold and the showroom converted into offices for the Morgan Law Partnership. The office housed a department of the local government administration.

HIGH STREET. *D.C.L.*
Following a statement in 1990 by Gerald Ratner that some of the products being sold were sub-standard, the Ratner shop on the corner of High Street and Crosswynd, was a clearance house for stock. The firm eventually ceased trading.

HIGH STREET. *D.C.L.*
James D. Bruce Ltd had a large retail bakery and tearoom on a site in the High Street that was taken over for an extension to Boots. Many of the businessmen in Dunfermline met in the restaurant every weekday morning for coffee. The photograph taken in the 1950s shows how shops closed and the entire shop staff gathered at the doorway to view the Children's Gala Day Parade.

HIGH STREET. *D.C.L. (E.M.C.)*

There are many photographs of the outside of F.W. Woolworth Stores but the company were reluctant to allow photography inside their shops, thus preventing imitation of their sales methods. Many shopping malls and retailers nowadays have a strict no photography policy. This photograph taken *c*.1954 shows the Dunfermline shop with its long counters and wooden floor. The shop was modernised in the 1960s and escalators installed between ground and first floors. New owners of the Woolworth Company in Britain deemed the building to be a saleable asset and the shop was closed. It remained closed for a number of years before being occupied by Goldbergs and subsequently Poundstretcher.

EAST PORT. *D.P.G.*

Elena Mae were retailers of photographic and hi-fi equipment and originally occupied a shop in High Street. They later took over the former radio and TV premises of A.L. Paterson in East Port. In the 1979 photograph manageress Christine Hutchison, is being presented with a sales award by area manager, Brian Blackmore. Brian has operated as an independent photographic retailer in his Bridge Street shop for the past 15 years.

HIGH STREET. *D.C.L.*

James Scott and Company was an electrical contractor, founded in Dunfermline, with branches in many towns in Scotland. They adopted a policy of opening large showrooms selling electrical appliances, radio, TV and hi-fi equipment in competition with the Electricity Boards. The property in the High Street was purchased because the shop that they already had in Queen Anne Street could not be extended. Work on the new project was not fully under way in 1953 when the coronation of the Queen took place but some effort has been put in to decorate the premises for this occasion.

CAMPBELL STREET. *D.C.L. (E.M.C.)*

While this photograph is not strictly taken post-war it is the only one available of the garage premises in use by the GPO for the red mail vans and green vehicles of the telephone engineers until the late 1970s.

BRUCE STREET. *D.C.L.*
A view of the entrance to Bruce Street in the 1950s as a
Co-operative fruit and vegetable cart squeezes past a
parked van. Parking was allowed on opposite sides of
the street on alternate days at this time. Burton's shop
and the entrance to the New Victoria restaurant can be
seen on the right and a sign for Kyle's premises is above
the parked van.

BRUCE STREET. *D.C.L.*
The photograph shows one of the daily hazards in
Bruce Street in the early 1950s when it was still open to
two-way traffic. The large furniture van of Wm.
Stevenson and Sons had to be reversed into the shop
loading bay while pedestrians had to look to their own
safety.

BRUCE STREET. *D.C.L.*
Peter Leslie, photographer and retailer of photographic equipment, Wm Stevenson and Sons, auctioneers and furniture retailers, with a department that stocked prams and cots, McKissock, retailers and repairers of radio and TV sets, two public houses and numerous small shops meant that Bruce Street was a popular and busy street in the late 1950s when this photograph was taken. One-way traffic had been introduced but there were still no yellow lines.

BRIDGE STREET. *D.C.L.*
A view of Bridge Street in the early 1950s shows traffic travelling in the opposite direction to that of today. Parking is on opposite sides of the street on alternate days. The shops of David Hutton and Son on one side and Bruce and Glen, just visible, on the other together with Hoy's furniture shop can be seen.

BRIDGE STREET. *D.C.L.*

With the exception of the new shop premises built for Mothercare on the south side of the street the properties have changed little in 30 years as this photograph *c*.1980 shows. David Hutton and Son still occupy their imposing premises but many other shops have new names above them. The window display in the shop adjacent to Hutton's shows that Donald the Draper has relocated to the former Coull and Matthew shop from the premises at Appin Crescent.

CARNEGIE STREET. *D.C.L.*

The widening of Carnegie Street and the formation of a four-lane road leading to a new road junction at Appin Crescent when it was renamed Carnegie Drive, saw the demolition of these houses on the north side of the street in the photograph taken *c*.1960. The small lorry is exiting from a lane that led to the fire station yard and to Mitchell's lemonade works. The building on the right of the photograph was originally built as a bonded warehouse for Bruce and Glen with a public hall above that doubled as a roller skating rink. The hall later was divided to become the Salvation Army Hall and manufacturing premises for Philip and Murray, embroiderers and cloth finishers, and was used for these purposes until the late 1950s. The premises have since been used as a clothing warehouse by Patrick Murray, a furniture store by Thomson and as restaurant premises by a number of owners. It is now an upmarket bar and restaurant.

CHALMERS STREET. *D.C.L. (W. Clark)*
Shortly after this photograph was taken in 1962, the Chalmers Street Church, by this time a Masonic Hall, would be demolished to allow the formation of an entrance to the new car park created when the ravine of the Town Burn was filled in. Bernstein's Furniture Arcade would be occupied by McPherson's bookshop when it relocated from the Regal Close. At this time there were a number of 'Iron Cows' located around Dunfermline. These were coin-operated machines, suitably refrigerated, from which cartons of milk could be purchased. One can be seen outside the office and showroom premises of Hunter and Wyse, plumber.

EAST PORT. *D.C.L. (E.M.C.)*
In 1981 the Dunfermline Building Society occupied two mansion houses linked by a banking hall. The premises were proving to be too small for the rapidly expanding society and a new headquarters and branch building was being erected on the former St Margaret's Parish Church. The scaffolding on the building site at the far end of the street is visible on the photograph. The wool and toyshops of Kay Bruce on either side of the entrance of the dental surgery of Sandy Mitchell are on the right.

CROSSWYND. *D.C.L.*

The photograph taken *c.*1971 shows Crosswynd still open to traffic. Nicol's, gents' outfitters, occupied the prominent site on the corner opposite that of the North of Scotland Bank. In the roadway can be seen the cobbles which marked the site of the Mercat Cross when it was rebuilt in the corner of the pavement at the Guildhall. It returned to its traditional site after the completion of the pedestrianisation of the High Street in 1992.

NEW ROW. *D.C.L.*

This 1960s photograph of the top of the New Row shows the range of shops situated there. On the right corner is the specialist food and wine shop of D.I. Hunter with Goldbergs and a Dunfermline Co-operative branch shop further down the hill. On the left-hand side of the street is a small millinery shop followed by the Hobby and Model Shop, the electrical appliance and radio workshop of James Scott and Co. and beyond the office block and Masonic Hall can be seen the display of Kirkhope, later Somerville, the photographer. The 'No Waiting' sign on the pavement is to reserve space for deliveries to the cellars of the East Port Bar.

HIGH STREET. *D.C.L.*

The junction of High Street, Guildhall Street and Crosswynd is not very busy on this wet day in the early 1950s. The Woolworth store is obviously the place to be for warmth and shelter judging by the crowd of people in the doorway. The signs on the lamp standard indicate the location of the car park in St Margaret's Street and, more importantly, the location of the Queen Anne Street toilets, described as Toilet Rooms. As can be seen on the photograph there was two-way traffic in the High Street at this time.

HIGH STREET. *D.C.L.*

This end of the High Street was dominated by the premises of the Dunfermline Co-operative Society on the right of this early 1950s photograph. John Scott, Butcher, is on the left and beyond that is Nairn's furniture store in the former Woolworth 3d and 6d store, now Thomson's. The two-way traffic in Bridge Street, which also operated in the High Street, can be seen. One test for Boy Scouts was to name all of the businesses down one side of the street and up the other.

HIGH STREET. *D.C.L.*

The adverts for Halloween Cakes in the window of Martin the Bakers show that the photograph was probably taken in October 1969. The Regal Cinema Restaurant has acquired a cocktail bar. Several old established Dunfermline businesses such as Shepherd the Butcher, Lambert the Hatter and Thomson the Watchmaker and Jeweller are still in evidence. The Town Council Street Lighting Department has started to erect the Christmas lights for which Dunfermline was famous.

DUNFERMLINE CO-OPERATIVE SOCIETY. *D.C.L.*

A series of photographs was taken for the Society in 1954 showing the staff and management at that time. The ladies of the Check Office had to meticulously record the figures from every sales check issued by every branch and department of the society. The dividend declared, which could be as much as 2s 6d in the pound, was then paid out based on these figures. Most customers did not retain the check receipts that they were given but some did and were prepared to challenge the staff if the figures did not tally and if the customer thought that they had been underpaid, never overpaid. The dividend payment was quickly spent in the Co-operative stores and dividend would be accrued on these purchases. Everyone remembers their mother's Co-operative membership number that they had to recite every time they 'went for the messages' even although it is perhaps 60 years since they last said it.

DUNFERMLINE CO-OPERATIVE SOCIETY. *D.C.L.*
Male members of staff were also photographed in 1954 and many well-known branch managers and department heads can be recognised.

DUNFERMLINE CO-OPERATIVE SOCIETY. *D.C.L.*
The Mutuality Club staff in 1954 was responsible for the smooth running of what was an early form of hire purchase. Customers started a savings account that then entitled them to make purchases in excess of what they had saved. While they were paying off one lot of purchases they could be adding more, thus binding them to the scheme and making them loyal Co-operative customers. The dividend was sometimes used to pay off Mutuality Club debts.

DUNFERMLINE CO-OPERATIVE SOCIETY. *D.C.L. (N)*
The large-scale development on the east side of Randolph Street in 1961 was named Unitas House. It included this restaurant and function room that extended the capacity and facilities of the Unitas Hall built in 1926.

DUNFERMLINE CO-OPERATIVE SOCIETY.
D.C.L. (E.M.C.)
The Wines and Spirits Department of the Co-operative Society was located in the former premises of the boot and shoe repairers in West Queen Anne Street, Rotten Row, and naming it the Cobbler was an obvious choice. It remained there with Ray Thomson as manager until it was moved to the Randolph supermarket to allow the building to be demolished and the site redeveloped.

DUNFERMLINE CO-OPERATIVE SOCIETY. *D.P.G.*
This is the supermarket that never was. It was built on the site of the former St Andrew's Parish Church and various co-operative properties in 1988 but never opened its doors for business. The Dunfermline Co-operative society was taken over by Co-operative Retail Services who decided that the building did not meet their standards. All of the shops in the Randolph Street complex closed two years later.

LOOKING FORWARD

The City and Royal Burgh of Dunfermline has undergone many changes in its 1,000-year history. The first 600 saw the demise of its dominance as a monastic centre and its favoured status as a royal residence making it just another Scottish town. The past 60 years have witnessed the loss of three major sources of employment and wealth, coal mining, linen weaving and the Rosyth naval dockyard. The result of this could have been a time of depression pushing Dunfermline into the backwaters of Scottish life. Instead, new industries have been lured to the area and their diversity should ensure that the prosperity of Dunfermline is no longer dependent on one or two major employers.

The 21st century will probably see expansion of Dunfermline to the west with the plans for the development of the fields of Urquhart Farm being revived. New and improved transport links with Edinburgh will probably see the building of another river crossing at Queensferry. The opening of the railway to Stirling, Alloa and the west together with the new bridge at Kincardine will make commuting to and from these areas easier. Who knows, the shopping development that will replace the former Co-operative complex may be completed.

There are ambitious plans to redevelop Pittencrieff Park and to promote it as the number one visitor attraction in the area.

History and heritage will be emphasised with the installation of new plaques on the places of importance. This, together with improved signage, guidebooks and floodlighting, should attract visitors to Dunfermline. The theme, 'Royal Dunfermline' is now being actively promoted.

The ferry service from Zeebruge to Rosyth should allow Dunfermline to become as popular to visitors from the Continent as Ghent and Bruges are to visitors from Scotland. Only time will tell.